Gwen

Unless you believe
you will not understand

Zen

AND THE ART OF
Falling in Love

BRENDA SHOSHANNA, PH.D.

Simon & Schuster Paperbacks
New York London Toronto Sydney

SIMON & SCHUSTER PAPERBACKS
Rockefeller Center
1230 Avenue of the Americas
New York, NY 10020

This Simon & Schuster paperback edition 2005

SIMON & SCHUSTER PAPERBACKS and colophon are registered
trademarks of Simon & Schuster, Inc.

For information about special discounts for bulk purchases,
please contact Simon & Schuster Special Sales at
1-800-456-6798 or business@simonandschuster.com.

Designed by Bonni Leon

Manufactured in the United States of America

10   9

The Library of Congress has cataloged the hardcover edition as follows:

Shoshanna, Brenda.
    Zen and the art of falling in love / Brenda Shoshanna.
        p.   cm.
    1. Spiritual life—Zen Buddhism.   2. Zen Buddhism—Doctrines.
    3. Love—Religious aspects—Zen Buddhism.   I. Title.
    BQ9288 .S546   2003
    294.3'444—dc21   2002191226

ISBN-13: 978-0-7432-4335-3
ISBN-10:   0-7432-4335-8
ISBN-13: 978-0-7432-4336-0 (Pbk)
ISBN-10:   0-7432-4336-6 (Pbk)

I dedicate this book

to the beauty and sparkle

of three precious children

who naturally know and

continually live a life of love—

Zoe, Remy and

Jacob Benjamin

Acknowledgments

I WISH TO ACKNOWLEDGE the wonderful help and unfailing support of my agent, Noah Lukeman, who is a guiding light behind all I do. I also wish to extend special thanks to my excellent editor, Amanda Murray, for her enthusiastic and lively interest in this work. I thank my wonderful brother Danny, who has listened to my endless stories about love, for his amazing endurance and loving patience.

Special thanks to the wonderful years of Zen training provided by Soen Roshi and Eido Roshi and to the blessed heart of Rabbi Joseph Gelberman, whose entire life is dedicated to love.

Special thanks are offered for the unending concern and love of family and close friends, especially to Gerry, Leah, Melissa, Abram, Joshua, Yana, Adam, Taisan, and to Jeff Azbell, Yoshi Amakawa, Jacques Van Engel, Fran Perillo, Carolyn Stark and Stuart Schwartz.

Contents

Part Three

ADVANCED TRAINING   157

Introduction

> We never ask the meaning of life
> when we are in love.
> —BHAGWAN SHREE RAJNEESH

WE ARE MEANT TO LIVE A LIFE of love. When we're not in love, something's the matter. Unfortunately, most of us become resigned to disappointment, loss and upset in relationships. No matter how successful we are in other aspects of our lives, most of us don't feel naturally entitled to the same success in love. "Being realistic about relationships" is considered natural as we "grow up" and give up the fantasies, foolishness and dreams of childhood. But nothing could be further from natural. The fantasies, foolishness and confused expectations we develop as we grow older are precisely what put us into a state of paralysis. We don't realize that when we are not in love, something's wrong.

Being in love is the most mature and realistic thing you can do. It energizes your life, fills you with positivity, creates generosity and makes every moment beautiful. Being in love immediately dispels the sense of purposelessness and disconnection that many grapple with. The body heals, the heart is happy.

Being in love is our natural state. The real question we should be asking is, why *aren't* we in love all the time? What is it that keeps this most precious inheritance away? How can we reclaim it for our own and return to the intrinsic wisdom and spontaneity we had as children, when each moment was fresh and exciting and filled with adventure?

Contrary to popular opinion, real love never hurts or wounds. Only our confused expectations can undermine our lives and lead us to negative consequences. There is a Buddhist saying: "Give up poisonous food wherever it is offered to you." Once we know what is poison and what is nourishing in our relationships, once we learn the laws of love and how to practice them, we will be able to live a life of love and build relationships that cannot fail. Zen shows how we can turn our lives around at any time.

There are two different schools of Zen training: Rinzai Zen and Soto Zen. Rinzai Zen emphasizes koan study, breaking through the barriers that keep our life force tied in knots. Soto Zen emphasizes the application of Zen to everyday life. Although training in both schools goes on in a zendo (a place where Zen meditation and other forms of practice are taught), the fruits of practice appear in our lives and relationships. Both Rinzai and Soto practice are included in this book.

Zen practice offers us an entirely different way of looking at love and relationships. In Zen practice we learn how to make friends with every aspect of ourselves and others—

nothing is rejected, nothing is left out. We return to basics and become able to distinguish between real needs and false ones. In Zen one learns to sit, to breathe, to focus, to let go, to walk with attention, to cook, to clean, to receive blows and to be prepared for intense and intimate encounters. As we do this cravings, addictions, fears and compulsions of all kinds slowly dissolve.

Zen and love are incredibly compatible. The wonderful, ancient practice of Zen is actually the practice of falling in love. When one focuses on and welcomes all that life brings, each day becomes a good day in which you are able to fall in love with all of life, to continually find wonder, kindness, friendship and playfulness.

The book is divided into three parts and each part offers new building blocks to help you prepare to love and have a deeper understanding of love itself.

Part I, "Starting Out," emphasizes the initial steps we take in Zen practice. Not only does it explain the specifics of what a Zen student learns (including how to do Zen meditation), but it also shows how these steps apply to relationships and how they help prepare an individual to know himself more fully, release control and become available to love.

Part II, "Zen in Action," describes the ways in which the focus and insight attained in meditation is then transferred to all our actions and to our everyday lives. We see how Zen principles—such as emptying yourself, being there for others, taking new steps and dealing with blows—are crucial building blocks in developing and maintaining loving relationships.

Part III, "Advanced Training," takes us to the top of the mountain. As training progresses the individual develops the ability to deal with moments of intense confrontation, decision, conflict and the need for endurance through difficult times. As training advances and the student gains an entirely new awareness of herself and the world around her, she finally becomes able to "meet the beloved," to experience the essence of love.

In each part readers will learn new means of dealing with the usual trouble spots in relationships, such as miscommunication, lies, betrayal, jealousy, insecurity, boredom, feelings of worthlessness, loss and disappointment. As readers look at these issues through the eyes of Zen practice, they receive life-changing perspectives, instructions and outcomes.

Although Zen practice is simple, it is not always easy. The reader is asked to suspend judgment and disbelief, to be willing to become a child once again—to explore, play, hug, cry and feel that the world is filled with endless possibilities, which it is, once you are willing to see it that way. Zen also requires the ability to say no to all of the people, beliefs, habits and desires that can take your faith and love away. Falling in love doesn't mean being blind or entering into fantasy. It means waking up out of darkened dreams to finally see the beauty that surrounds us.

This book is not only for those who wish to experience

loving relationships, but also for those who wish to be able to enjoy their lives to the fullest. It is an invitation onto this wonderful path. A little endurance is required, along with the willingness to face the shadows that will dispel as soon as we invite in the light.

Part One

STARTING OUT

Chapter 1

TAKING OFF YOUR SHOES
(becoming available)

I'd like to offer something
to help you.
But in the Zen school
We don't have a single thing.
—IKKYU

WE ALL WANT LOVE. We are all searching for love, searching for some lasting relationship. Yet it always seems as if relationships are difficult—difficult to find, to keep and to
enjoy. But the fundamental truth is that there is no inherent
problem with relationships at all. There is never a scarcity of
relationships, there is never a scarcity of love. Love is our
natural condition. Why aren't we in it all the time? What
keeps us from this love we are so hungry for?

The usual answer to this question is that there are no

good men or women around. No matter who we meet, something is wrong. No matter what kind of relationship we develop, something starts to go awry. In the beginning we may feel we have finally found the perfect person. Then before we know it, often out of the blue, conflict develops, irritation grows. Joy, pleasure and excitement, the feeling of being loved and valued, fade imperceptibly. Most people have no idea why this happens.

When some individuals have bitter or disappointing experiences in love, they sometimes shut down and become determined not to risk anything again. They grow numb and hardened, looking past every person they meet.

Disappointment in love is routine, everyday business. A large percentage of therapists' patients report disappointment in love. Some therapists go back to their patients' childhoods, unravel their disappointments in love and see how they then project these feelings upon the people they now meet. Others examine the ways in which individuals talk to themselves about the people they meet, and about themselves. They teach different ways to think and speak about love and work with "self-esteem." Some therapists teach new interpersonal skills, make their patients better at communication, show them how to choose their partners differently, to take responsibility for their shortcomings. The ultimate goal of these methods is to have their patients find someone they can be happy with and settle down with. There is nothing wrong with any of these methods.

Ultimately, though, from the psychological point of view, not falling in love, in and of itself, is not a symptom of great pathology. In fact, some patients can do very well, become quite healthy, and yet never get over their disappointments in love. They may never be able to develop satisfying, primary love relationships, but there are many ways to have other meaningful relationships, a productive work life, other interests and experience a satisfying life.

Is a person's very life at stake if she isn't able to truly love? Some would not put it so drastically, but the Zen answer is yes. According to Zen, without the ability to know real love, the precious taste of this life is thwarted.

TAKE OFF YOUR SHOES: A ZENDO LESSON

Zen is not excitement, but concentration on our usual everyday routine.
—SHUNRYU SUZUKI, *ZEN MIND, BEGINNER'S MIND*

During the course of Zen training, students receive various instructions. Each instruction contains the essence of Zen, and must be followed completely and carefully. At the heart of this practice is the willingness to do everything 100 percent, to consider nothing to be too big or too small. As we do this, we soon realize that even our tiniest actions are reflective of who we are and affect our entire life.

When a student first comes to the *zendo* (the Zen training center), she usually has no idea what to expect. The first thing that might strike her when she opens the door could be the pungent smell of incense, the deep silence, the immaculately clean, shining wooden floors or how open and empty the place is, with everything exactly where it belongs. After she walks in, the first instruction she will receive is a simple one, "Take off your shoes." She has no choice but to do what is asked of her. Otherwise, she cannot come in.

In Zen practice we become exposed. When we take off our shoes, we begin the process of letting go of our usual defenses and external signs of value. In the zendo we find our true value, and for that we must first open up and let go of that which we cling to. As we do so, we find that what we have been clinging to is what causes the conflict and pain. As practice continues, it becomes easier to take off our shoes and walk, exposed and barefoot along a wooden floor. We learn to do what is asked of us without hesitation and may even notice that our inability to have done so in the past contributed to our former experiences of disappointment and rejection in love.

The first step in Zen practice is not to disregard anything, including one's shoes. Usually we pay little attention to the world we live in, just as we pay little attention to our shoes. We take everything for granted. Zen practice changes this. As we practice, we realize that everything is significant— every little moment, everything we do. The beginning of practice is to take off our shoes mindfully, to appreciate them for what they are, what they have been giving us. Then we learn how to place them in such a manner that they will not interfere with the atmosphere of the room. Messy shoes create a chaotic environment, and a chaotic environment creates confused, angry people. As a Zen master says:

> Once a newcomer is barefooted, they will enter the zendo. Many walk in nonchalantly, sauntering or gazing around. A Zen student will stop them.
> "Pay attention to the bottom of your feet."
> The newcomer may be startled.
> "Your feet are precious," the Zen student will repeat.
> "Pay attention to them when you walk."

Sauntering or being concerned with the impression you are creating isn't necessary in Zen practice. Instead, in the zendo, one must simply pay attention to one's feet. Our feet are amazing. They contain endless nerve endings that can give us incredible information about the place we are in, about ourselves, our lives and our direction. Our feet can also assist greatly in coming to balance. Without balance and accurate information, how are loving relationships possible? Yet how many of us take the time to pay attention to our own balance and wisdom, to the bottom of our own feet?

In one sense, each instruction in Zen training is a metaphor for our entire lives, an instruction to diligently follow and practice day by day. By simply paying attention to each step that we take, by becoming that attentive and present, we can turn around our relationships.

PLANTING NEW SEEDS

In Zen we speak a great deal about cause and effect. Our lives, our karma, are seen as the ripening of a chain of seeds we have planted. When poisonous seeds are planted, a sickly tree grows. Sometimes this seed has been planted years ago, before we can remember, but nevertheless, when conditions are ready, the fruit of the seed is sure to appear. When we look for love and cannot experience it, the effect of our hungry, messy karma may be ripening. By taking our attention back to ourselves, to the way we treat the world and, indeed, to all our actions, big and small, we begin to take charge of the seeds we are planting now. We will not have to roam around in the world looking for love we cannot ever have.

HUNGRY GHOSTS

An individual who cannot love may be doomed to live her days as a "hungry ghost." Hungry ghosts are individuals who are starving. Even though they are led to tables spread with endless food and precious delights, no matter how much they eat they cannot be satisfied. They aren't able to taste the food, so no matter how much they put in their mouths, they continue to search for more.

Hungry ghosts might sample one relationship after the next, not knowing how to digest it. They never know who the person is in front of them, or who they are themselves. All they know is that they want more and more. They fantasize that someone else, the perfect person, is about to walk in the door. Certain hungry ghosts appear available for love, but they are really only intent on seducing and teasing the people they find. As soon as love is demanded from them, they reject the person. Their pleasure is in withdrawing the love they seem to be offering. This provides these individuals a sense of control, so that nobody will ever control them through this strange experience of love.

Hungry ghosts are the people who enter huge rooms filled with single people and immediately say, "There's no one here tonight." They cannot experience or be satisfied with that which life presents. In terms of relationships, they go around and around on the merry-go-round, grabbing for the gold ring, always just beyond their grasp, or if they do catch it, they soon discover to their horror that it is not true gold, but brass.

All of this is exhausting and disheartening and makes the hungry ghosts very sad. Even when they are with someone they love, they are often haunted by the notion that their true soul mate is somewhere else, eluding them. Their painful affliction, which has become quite common, can be remedied through the practice of Zen. In Zen practice they are taught to be fully present to each moment, not run this way and that.

SEEKING A DREAM

Rachel, thirty-three, an attractive, single woman, dated relentlessly, seeking a satisfying love. No matter how well things started out in the beginning, eventually her relationships fell apart. Although she did her best to be charming and pleasing, most of the time the men became unresponsive, then boring or irritating to her. Rachel found something wrong with all of them and soon decided that nothing they did could please or satisfy her. Not one of them resembled the image of the partner she had in her mind, the one she was looking for. Before long she resented the time and energy she'd been spending with these individuals and looked for a way to get out.

After the initial excitement and high hopes of the beginning of the relationship, these continual letdowns not only drained Rachel, but began to increasingly depress her. Many days she found herself despairing of ever finding love. She felt she left these relationships with less than when she started. They made her feel even more empty and alone. Soon she began to wonder if there wasn't something wrong with her.

Rachel was not able to really know or be with the person

she was dating. She had so many dreams and expectations of how the man had to be. The men, who sensed this, withdrew. Rather than seeing her part in this process, rather than realizing she was seeking a dream, Rachel judged and blamed them all. It was no wonder her relationships could never be fulfilling. She had yet to absorb the wonderful Zen teaching:

Praise and blame, away with them once and for all.

When Rachel embarks upon Zen practice, she will focus upon what is before her, and will not be allowed to dwell upon passing fantasies. She will also learn to do what is needed, not necessarily to lead a life where her own personal wishes are paramount. Rachel will come to see that, indeed, this is what has been preventing her from enjoying relationships, from realizing exactly who she is with and how to honor and receive them. Slowly, she will give up her demands and judgments, and in the process free herself.

When Rachel learns to take off her shoes carefully and to place her attention on each step she takes, she will leave her defenses and constrictions behind and come to discover that everything we do affects not only ourselves, but others as well. She may even ask herself what she has really been offering to the men she has been dating. Although she doesn't yet realize it, she had been discarding one man after the next, tossing them mindlessly away. There are many reasons love may not be flourishing in our lives, and a messy, demanding mind is reason one.

GETTING WHAT WE WANT

Whatever we are in life, we bring to the zendo. When we first enter we may expect to come in and immediately find a way to get our needs met, or become quickly enlightened, meaning that everything will magically work out fine, just the way we want it to. Nothing can be further from the truth.

We have been programmed to believe that if we get what we want, we are a success. We want excitement, change, pleasure, stimulation, good friends, praise and happy conversation. We want to go home feeling that we have done beautifully, that others respect and appreciate that. This is also what we want from relationships. As we undergo Zen training, we learn how to turn self-centered, negative desires around. In fact, after we take off our shoes, one of the first things we have to learn is how to deal with not getting what we want at all.

THE ROOT OF OUR PAIN

Zen teaches us not to deal with the branches of confusion that cause a person to reject love, but instead go to the root of the illness and pull out the sick tree itself. Once the root is gone, pain and confusion cannot sprout any longer. Now there is room for a new tree to grow, one that bears rich, delicious fruit. Coming from a healthy root, individuals who start a "good relationship" will find it does not disappear after a period of time. They do not need to run to a therapist and ask why love has vanished, or what is wrong with the other person or with themselves. They realize, finally, that nothing is wrong with either themselves or with anyone. Suddenly, no more problems exist.

Until we realize this, we are bound to search for what we think we need somewhere outside ourselves. Our entire search for happiness, comfort, value and meaning is directed to the external world because we believe that this is where happiness lies. We want to grab a chunk of it for ourselves, and then we want to hold on tight.

But when the external world is constantly changing, how can we hold on to it tightly? Once we have it up close, we realize it is never what we have imagined, neither as beautiful nor as ugly. The external world comes, goes and changes; that is its very nature. To search for contentment and stability in a world of changes can only lead to disappointment and sorrow.

Sometimes the search for someone "out there" to love yields someone exciting, but inevitably, both the person and the feelings we have for them change—they have to. We interpret this as failure. But there is no such thing as failure in real love.

As soon as Rachel begins to practice, she will be starting the process of taking back her scattered energies, discovering how to extricate herself from traps and truly fall in love. As Rachel begins to take her shoes off mindfully, control her messy mind, listen to what is being asked of her and respect the needs and wishes of others, she will begin taking responsibility for the effects of her own actions upon others. Soon she will begin to realize the ways in which she has been inviting or repelling love. As she does this Rachel will be planting new seeds from which new blossoms will inevitably sprout. It takes many years to realize what both love and Zen practice are, and how to become a beginning student. This process requires patience. But without patience we have nothing. Developing patience is at the very heart of our ability to love.

When we judge a person quickly and discard him because he does not meet a preconceived notion we have, we are short-circuiting our own ability to find love. When we have the patience to allow time for who he truly is to be revealed, there will be many surprises and we will be expanding the circle of people who may enter our lives.

In a similar vein, when we are in a relationship that started out beautifully and it begins to go through a difficult time, we must realize that this is the natural course of many relationships and does not necessarily mean it's time to leave. Develop the patience to wait until the choppy waters have stilled and you can both see clearly what's really going on.

DEVELOPING PATIENCE

Love without patience is like soup without liquid—impossible to drink. It can even be said that patience is love itself. In the frantic, demanding world Rachel lives in, patience has been relegated to a shadow of the past. She never allowed the time for love to develop. As soon as she was upset, she fled from the relationship; she could not tolerate her own emptiness or the perceived emptiness of others.

But patience is greatly needed for the flower of love to bloom. It takes time for a person to feel at home in a relationship and to reveal who she is. It takes patience to wait for another, to develop true caring and trust.

Hungry ghosts, however, have a difficult time with patience. Starving for food and love, they will often grab at anything just to satisfy themselves. Some don't even know the difference between food and garbage—they'll take it in anyway, just as long as they can immediately feel full. It's that hollow feeling they can't tolerate that drives their lives. Through Zen Rachel will learn how to wait and distinguish between empty and real food. No one will tell her how to do this. She will not receive ready-made solutions but will have to grapple with the experiences of her life directly, taste them, digest them and discover what they mean for her.

Zen practice is based upon contradiction and paradox. As students endure deprivation and other hardships, warmth, clarity and flexibility arise. They grow to understand that without the willingness to endure and practice, nothing real can happen. Life and love happen in a second, and yet it takes preparation to be ready to receive them.

Stepping-Stones to Love Developing Mindfulness

These processes can be done daily, hourly, monthly or yearly. It's up to you. Don't turn them into another pressure. Make them something life-giving that you can enjoy.

1. TAKE OFF YOUR SHOES
Take off your shoes carefully, mindfully, with real attention. Place them neatly where they belong. Be aware of yourself as you do this, and be aware of them. Day by day, build a relationship with your shoes. Value and care for them. See how they feel the next morning when you put them on again. This practice of mindful attention will help begin the process of opening up.

2. SPEND TIME NOTICING
Spend time noticing what needs to be taken care of. Is it a thirsty plant in your apartment? Are your bills paid? Are there letters left unanswered, people waiting to be called back? At this point just notice these things, and notice your willingness—or lack of willingness—to do what is needed.

3. LOOK OVER PAST RELATIONSHIPS
Give time and attention to looking over past relationships. Just look. Don't blame yourself for what happened, and

don't blame anyone else. Just become quiet and look over the people, places and events. Write down what you notice. Let it all be as it was. In the days that follow see if what happened in past relationships is cropping up in the present. Don't make anything of it. Just notice the patterns as you would notice a rainbow in the sky.

This process of watching, noticing, paying attention is very powerful. It is at the heart of Zen. We pass so much of our days under the thick fog of absentmindedness, fantasy and resentment, that it may come as a shock to see the effect of our caring attention, which makes room for the sun of clarity to shine in.

4. THE ONE BESIDE YOU NOW

Look at a person who is close to you right now—anyone it happens to be. Notice the ways in which you push him away. Stop doing that for a moment. Become aware of what he is offering and what he is not. Allow the two of you to be together in whatever way you are. Just be with it all for a little while and let it be fine the way it is.

Do the same thing tomorrow with someone else. We discount so many people who are in our worlds, while waiting for "the right one" to appear.

> Sometimes we have the power to say yes to life.
> Then peace enters us and makes us whole.
> —RALPH WALDO EMERSON

Chapter 2

SITTING ON THE CUSHION
(meeting yourself)

Do not look at the faults of others.
Look at your own deeds, done and undone.
—BUDDHA

MOST OF US YEARN FOR OUR "perfect mate" and start our quest for him feeling sure he's out there, waiting for us somewhere. In the beginning, there isn't anything we won't do to find him. We search fervently, making lists of qualities we want him to have and creating pictures of the way life will be when he's at our side. We are firmly convinced that when we find the right person, happiness will be a short step away.

And yet, very often, soon after someone who seems to fit the bill arrives and a relationship is started, much to our amazement and horror, he turns into someone else—someone quite familiar, often a repeat of past relationships. When this happens more than once, we become emotionally shaky and begin to doubt our judgment.

Although we don't realize it, this *doubting* is good. It's the beginning of a new way of perceiving. Our usual judgment *should* be doubted. Whether or not we like it, we are born and live in the grip of dreams and illusions.

Many of us refuse to see the people standing before us (including ourselves) for who they really are. Instead, we seek the thrill, glamour and false comfort produced by fantasies, hoping that this new person will be the one we have been searching for, finally providing the unconditional love we are so desperate to receive. Although this has not happened in the past (or, if it did, was only short-lived), we live with the dream that *this* time will be different.

THE MYTH OF SISYPHUS

In the Greek myth, Sisyphus was doomed to roll a very heavy rock up a mountain. Right before he reached the top, the rock rolled back down again. Sisyphus then had to engage in the same effort, rolling the rock back up. His entire life was like this, mechanical, repetitive, empty of meaning or the gratification received from fulfilling a task. This is how many individuals begin to feel about relationships and the possibility of finding love. No matter how hard they try to roll the rock up the mountain (to find the right person), it rolls back down again.

From the Zen point of view, we must simply stop rolling the rock back up the mountain. We must break our attachment to mechanical patterns and the false notion that the love we so desperately crave comes from somewhere else. When we are dependent upon the external world to fulfill us, sooner or later the rock we have rolled up the mountain begins to fall down again. Conditions change, people leave, our sense of ourself falters with the changes wrought by time. As we undertake Zen practice, our ability to love and be loved develops from another basis.

SITTING DOWN: A ZENDO LESSON

In order to break out of our usual behavior we are instructed to "Sit down and stop moving." This is the basis of Zen meditation. We sit on the cushion with our spine straight, eyes down, hands in a special position and pay attention only to our breathing. When the sitting begins, when the bell rings out, we do not move no matter what we are feeling, until the sitting is over and the bell rings again. In this way we are forced to stop reacting blindly and learn to watch all that arises, both within and without.

When a newcomer arrives at the zendo, after taking off her shoes and leaving the rest of her baggage behind, she walks into the meditation hall and sits down. She walks slowly and carefully, holding on to nothing for comfort or support.

Before we can even approach the cushion, the great activity of "sitting down," we must disengage from the usual clutter and supports we cling to all day long. We turn away from the idea that the more we have the better; or the more we know, or the smarter, busier or more frantic we are, the more we are getting done. In the zendo we put our bundle down.

This entire process of disembarking, which may seem daunting, is easier than it seems. Rather than engaging in endless rumination about it, devising theories and speculating, we simply put our packages down. We hang up our coat and put whatever we have carried neatly in the space provided. Nothing further is required. As a great Zen master said, "Zen is simply picking up your coat from the floor and putting it where it belongs."

Zen is utterly simple and in that lies its power. Everybody and anybody has the ability to do it; nothing special is required, only a willingness to be who you are.

As the newcomer walks into the zendo a senior student will most likely yell, "Eyes on the floor!"

Although it may be difficult for a newcomer to resist her longing to check everyone out, she must keep her eyes down. Still, she may keep wondering what the others are doing here. Why had they all come anyway? Are they hopeless like her? Are they all just basically nuts? Is there someone she'd like? This scattered, distracted approach is exactly how most people behave when looking for a relationship.

THE WILD MONKEY MIND

The practice of *zazen* (Zen meditation) stops this frantic activity, quiets our wild monkey mind. Our wild monkey mind loves to accompany us wherever we go. It is an inner chorus of continual comment that spoils everything we meet and prevents us from truly being with whatever appears. An endless accompaniment to our lives, we take it to every person and relationship we encounter. Then we wonder why we have trouble falling in love.

When we enter a space such as the zendo that is plain, silent and open, this wild monkey mind may seem louder and fiercer. That is not the case, however. It's just that now, with the distractions gone, we can hear and realize what has been going on all along. The doors of awareness are opening a little. We may be amazed at what we find.

When Henry first came to the zendo he said, "I was so astonished by my violent, competitive comments on everything that was happening, that I almost fell off my seat. I was scared, dumbfounded. Who is this person living inside me? I wondered. Where did he come from? How long has he been living my life?"

Henry never understood why he couldn't progress in his love life. Sitting there on the cushion, he began to realize: If there was such fury raging inside me, how could he ever trust or be trusted by anyone? How could he know the next step to take?

By "just sitting," Henry grew sufficiently quiet and aware to be able to extricate himself from the turbulence within and become available to "just being" with someone else. In time he was ready for a relationship. This time it took a brand-new form.

DO IT ANYWAY

During initial instruction, a new student will be told to place her attention on her lower abdomen (*hara*), the space beneath the belly button. Once she is in the proper position she will be told to simply count her breaths from one to ten. When she gets to ten, it's back to one again, repeating the same thing. Nothing more, nothing less.

Although it sounds simple enough, many do not quite see the point of it.

"Do it anyway," the instructor will say.

Most of us enjoy understanding the reason behind every action we take and what the likely outcome will be. The same is true in relationships, where we need to understand exactly what is going on before we are willing to act.

In the zendo we act first and understand later. Our actions teach us all we need to know. Questions are beside the point; they are often simply distractions from the work at hand. The Buddha has said that we've all been shot with poison arrows. Rather than sit around and understand at what angle the arrow entered or what the poison is made of, we must quickly pull the arrow out. Time is of the utmost importance. We cannot delay.

"The more questions you ask," the instructor tells newcomers, "the farther away you'll be. Just sit courageously."

Just sit is a profound instruction. It is an instruction that takes many years to fulfill. In the beginning almost no one can do it. Almost no one can really accept instruction, become still, be with himself, expect nothing, just be willing to completely be there. The fervent search for love and acceptance in relationships is often simply an avoidance of this.

There seem to be so many ghosts in our closets, so much that we have pushed under the rug, refused to face about ourselves. When we sit on the cushion and simply pay attention to breathing, these ghosts (as well as many other things) begin to emerge all by themselves. We are opening the doors of our closet and letting the light in. We are not explaining, analyzing, seeking a solution—we are simply making acquaintance with our hopes, fears, idle thoughts. As we meditate, all energy used to hide from ourselves is now released to live our lives. All the secret fears, doubts and hatreds we may have accumulated bubble up, and then melt away, replaced by the compassion that is inevitably generated as we sit and breathe. This is an unexpected development, one that most people have no way of explaining.

THE WHEEL OF KARMA

In Zen we speak of the "wheel of karma," the notion that we can repeat the same relationships, have the same thoughts, take the same actions, receive the same consequences endlessly, from lifetime to lifetime (though we are not aware this is going on). In fact, many relationships we struggle with presently, we have been struggling with endlessly, and are now simply trying to make them work once again.

Nancy, twenty-eight, a beautiful, young professional woman, has everything exactly as she wants it, except her love life. She is open to meeting someone special—she is sure he exists—and dates frequently, sometimes as much as three times a week. She has no problem entering into new relationships, and in the beginning things are always great. But after a few months (or sometimes weeks) things seem to go sour. The men she meets, who are at first warm and affectionate, end up becoming distant and cold. They begin finding fault with her, just like her mother. Before she knows it, Nancy feels rejected again.

A psychologist might say that Nancy is in the grip of the "repetition compulsion," the need to repeat painful experiences and patterns in the hope that they will turn out right this time, which they never do. Her search for the perfect partner is a search to replace her mother, her original love object, who was cold and rejecting and who left Nancy feeling undeserving of love. Now she frantically searches for someone to love her, someone who will prove to her, finally, that she is worthwhile.

But if, because of childhood needs, we give others the power to decide our worthiness, we easily become ensnared in the grip of addictive relationships. These regressive relationships are upsetting and frustrating because they're based upon wanting to repair what happened in the past—not upon the realities of who we are now and what is truly available to us. By learning to sit, to not move or be reactive, Nancy would have an opportunity to stop the monkey mind that's been running her life, and take back her power for herself.

Carl, a young man Nancy was having a relationship with, also suffered from the same situation. When they started the relationship he thought she was beautiful, everything he'd ever been looking for. But as time passed he started to feel differently. She seemed less inviting, a little cold, and he became colder in return.

It is easy to see why Nancy and Carl attracted one another. They were both involved in the same dance and their matching karmic patterns made them feel they were in love. But in truth, this is the opposite of love. It is, in fact, the suffering of *samsara,* the endlessly repeating patterns of our daily lives. Unless "enlightenment" comes, unless we wake up to what is happening, develop awareness, learn to let go, our patterns, our karma, dictate our lives.

BREAKING KARMIC PATTERNS

As an individual embarks upon Zen practice, her karma immediately begins to change. When Nancy became a Zen student, she sat down quietly, straightening her back, crossing her legs and placing her hands in the proper position (called a *mudra*). Even on a neurological level, Nancy was now creating a circuit with her body of strength, balance and clarity. By keeping her back straight and not moving, she was causing random thoughts and feelings to decrease. She was saying no to the monkey mind, not following its wild dictates.

As Nancy continued sitting, at first her questions increased. However, little by little she stopped resisting the practice and began to become truly acquainted with herself. As this happened, her need for answers and approval from the outside diminished, as did her entrapment in the repetitive relationships she has been caught up in.

As Nancy undertook this practice regularly, her sense of doom began to fade away. Slowly she began to realize she was not in the grip of these repetitive patterns. By meeting them directly, their power over her diminished. As she sat, settled and aware, she also began to see that external validation was not so necessary. She could give compassion to herself.

In her next relationship, when the same pattern began to repeat, rather than feel doomed and withdraw, Nancy became quiet and observed what was going on. When the man became distant and cold, rather than take it personally, she recognized it for what it was—an old pattern repeating, not the truth of her value. As Nancy became less reactive to what was going on, the man's behavior changed as well. The two of them had an opportunity to behave differently with one another. Nancy also had an opportunity to decide if this was the right kind of man for her. New choices began to emerge. Out of the simple sitting, new worlds opened up.

As we "just sit," we are actually making friends with ourselves, finally willing to be with all of ourselves. We are willing to face whatever arises and not run away. Little by little, in this mysterious process, our fear of life and of our own being diminishes. We are not so pressured by inner compulsions—forced to live under the weight of karmic patterns that have no end. Needless to say, as we make acquaintance with ourselves, we are also getting to know the entire world. We don't have to race from person to person, or from situation to situation to know who's there or what's going on. The more we sit quietly and become connected to ourselves, the more the entire world unfolds before our eyes.

OPEN YOUR OWN TREASURE HOUSE

Daiju visited the master Baso in China. Baso asked, "What do you seek?"

"Enlightenment," replied Daiju.

"You have your own treasure house. Why do you search outside?" Baso asked.

Daiju inquired, "Where is my treasure house?"

Baso answered, "What you are asking is your treasure house."

Daiju was enlightened. Ever after he urged his friends: "Open your own treasure house and use those treasures."

When we sit, we open our own treasure house. Rather than do this, however, most of us first seek to find the treasures another person can provide. We calculate their value to us. When we approach relationships in this manner, we are coming as beggars, seeing the other as a source of supply. When we can enter a relationship with our treasure house already open, there is no end to the wonders we can find, both within and between ourselves and another.

HIDING IN ROLES AND GAMES

Another repetitive behavior many of us indulge in is playing familiar roles and games. We choose a persona—the sexy woman, the giver, the child, the powerhouse, the angel, the brat—that would be enticing to the lover we want. These roles help mask our reality. We strain to keep these roles going, and when we slip up and show our true selves, often love quickly fades away.

Sometimes we forget we're even playing a role, or fall in love with the fantasy and begin to believe it is who we truly are. Or, more commonly, we fall in love with someone else who is playing a role. Reality can come as quite a shock to us when the facade comes down and we are face to face with someone quite different.

We adapt personas to hide the parts of ourselves we cannot acknowledge. Ironically, these false egos are often exactly what keep us safe and secure in our loneliness.

Pretending to be strong, stoic, giving and always available can give us a sense of temporary security. Temporary security isn't bad, but it does not quell the inner turbulence. Sooner or later this turbulence emerges.

In the everyday world, sitting down and not moving, not running away, just silently making acquaintance with ourselves, may be considered foolish, dangerous—an indulgence, even. From the point of view of Zen practice, it is considered of the utmost importance, the fundamental activity needed before we can embark upon our lives. Without time spent in this manner our activities easily become confused, scrambled and frantic as we seek in the external world that which exists within.

Although sitting sounds simple, it is a profound action with enormous effects. As one begins to really sit, one becomes settled and calm, and can, for the first time, meet and value oneself. Without meeting ourselves, it is impossible to truly meet another. Soon the Zen student realizes that what she needs is not outside of herself. This is not a repudiation of other people or relationships, but an early step in preparing for a life of love.

The entry point is right where you are.
—ZEN SAYING

Stepping-Stones to Love
Becoming Aware of Repetitive Patterns

1. SIT DOWN

Stop what you are doing, put things aside, clear an empty space on the floor, place a cushion there and sit down. Straighten your back, cross your legs and follow your breath from one to ten. If you can do this for five minutes, do it. If you can do it longer, go ahead. Sit down without any expectations; just be with each breath as it comes and goes. Do this every day. If it is at all possible, do it in the daytime and evening.

2. REPETITIVE PATTERNS

Become aware of what is repetitive in your life—feelings, thoughts, relationships, patterns you struggle with. Just be aware of this. Also be aware of your repetitive struggle to solve these issues in the same old way. Don't blame or judge yourself for any of it. Notice everything about the repetitive cycles you are caught in. Let them be exactly as they are. Just add your kind and gentle awareness. (Take a moment and see how you would feel about a friend who had these patterns. Would you hate and judge her, or feel compassion?)

3. REPETITIVE RELATIONSHIPS

When you notice you are in a repetitive relationship, or a familiar pattern, stop yourself from reacting in the old way. Do not take what is happening personally. Do not fault the other, or run away. Become conscious that it is simply a pattern repeating. Become aware that you have other choices. Do something completely different from what you might have done before. Instead of becoming angry, extend kindness. Instead of hating yourself, focus upon all you have to offer. Instead of keeping old patterns going forever, engage in new activities and friendships right away.

4. WHO'S SITTING THERE?

We naturally have all kinds of ideas about who we are and aren't—what roles we play and what we don't, what about us is lovable and what is not. Take a few minutes out of the day, every day, to stop and notice, right at that moment, who you are being right now. We wear different hats as the day progresses and different demands are made of us. It is easy to get lost in a role, game or fantasy and completely forget who we are. It is easy to get lost trying to be all things to all people. Notice if you are doing that. (The more we sit, the more we become able to locate our true self each moment of the day.)

Now, notice what roles you play in relationships, and what roles you demand of the other. See if you are in love with the person, or with the role he is playing right now.

Turn this all upside down for a little while. Try playing different roles. Try being with someone who plays roles you are not accustomed to. Become aware of the difference between who you are and the roles you play.

5. HONORING OUR EFFORTS

It is natural to dwell upon our pain and difficulty and overlook the efforts and the steps we have taken. Find even a few very small things you have done today, and give yourself recognition for them. Honor your efforts toward the good, toward strength and becoming whole. Now do the same for someone else. Slowly you will learn to see your true nature and the true nature of others wherever you go.

> stopping,
> and counting every sound,
> stopping,
> and seeing every stone,
> stopping,
> and letting in the wind,
> stopping,
> and not having to be somebody
> —PETER ROSENGARDEN, AN ELEVEN-YEAR-OLD BOY

Chapter 3

DOING NOTHING
(releasing control)

If he comes we welcome,
If he goes we do not pursue.
—ZEN SAYING

WE ARE BORN WANTING TO CONTROL our world and the people in it. We scream to get food from Mother, smile to receive the attention we crave, pout at someone who is irritating and, when uncomfortable, resort to tantrums of all kinds. Implicitly, we feel that life must conform to our wishes, that others are here simply to keep us content. This kind of infantile attitude can be very hard to outgrow. In fact, it can be said that 99 percent of our precious life energy goes to manipulating the world so that it can fulfill our desires.

Just like the young baby, most of us have no real awareness of those around us. Others exist primarily as objects to fulfill our needs. The sense that they have lives of their own, dreams and desires that may be different from ours, perhaps even conflicting, is often too much to take in. What we call love in relationships is often no more than having someone who behaves in a way that makes us feel good. And if he doesn't do this, we'll resort to anything and everything to control him and change his ways.

In our culture, "looking out for number one" is considered normal, even healthy. We are taught to want to have it all, get our needs met, know how to maneuver successfully in relationships. When someone gets a good catch, shows off a big ring or some other sign of victory, she is praised by her peers and her status rises. When someone else has not been able to sustain a relationship she often feels inadequate and shamed. Our very identity is wrapped up with how well we can control our relationships, who we can get to "commit."

Many psychotherapies deal with this by trying to help individuals become more "successful in the world" by maneuvering better, being more able to get their personal desires fulfilled. However, we don't often take the time to examine the enormous stress and anxiety created by having to control others and oneself, by constantly having to produce in order to be of value, by always seeking to have one desire or another fulfilled.

All of this arises from the idea that it is up to us to carry both the world and our relationships on our shoulders. When something goes wrong, we blame ourselves, feeling there was something we left undone. One extra action could have changed everything. With this kind of orientation, we are always looking for the next thing to control, always living with a sense of imminent danger. In this state of mind, how is it possible to be in love?

Many people have no idea that there is an alternative way of living. They have not yet met the path of Zen. Zen practice is the opposite. It does not focus upon accumulation or attainment. It is not concerned with the way others see us. As we practice we become grateful and fulfilled by whatever we have. The Zen road to contentment comes from living from our true selves. And as Zen practitioners do this, paradoxically, their lives are often filled with wonderful activity, expression and attainment.

DON'T MOVE: A ZENDO LESSON

The only real miracle is to stand still.
—HENRY MILLER

In order to give up our frantic need to control ourselves, others and everything around us, Zen practice instructs us, "Don't move." Sit without moving until the bell rings. Whatever happens during the sitting, both within and without, maintain your posture. You are stronger than the endless irritants, delusions and distractions that seek to take your peace away. Nobody ever died on the cushion. No matter how you are feeling, your breath still comes and goes regularly. Pay attention to that.

Usually we move (and react) all the time. When something bothers us, we shift, change our position, do anything we can to fix it. Although our behavior alters the condition for a little while, it usually comes back again, sometimes more intensely, sometimes in another form. No matter what action we undertake, the irritation persists. No matter what action we take in relationships, at times there is nothing that will cause the trouble to go away.

In zazen (Zen meditation), by not moving we are surrendering control over the condition, we are allowing things to be as they are, to appear, develop, disappear, reappear in any way they may. We allow the entire world of phenomena to play itself out in front of our eyes. What we are learning to do is to profoundly let go of the need to control.

Don't move is a profound instruction, both in zazen and in relationships. It implies an immense respect for the intrinsic nature of people and events, for a larger design inherent in the universe that brings our good to us, and removes that which no longer belongs. How often we try to grasp and hold on to that which is no longer suitable, or to desperately maneuver to obtain that which may be entirely wrong. When we do not move, we are yielding to a higher wisdom, we are allowing life to take its own course.

LET EACH MOMENT BE AS IT IS

> The universe is sacred.
> You cannot improve it.
> If you try to change it, you will ruin it.
> If you try to hold it, you will lose it.
>
> —LAO-TZU

Basically we are only guests for a short time upon this beautiful earth. How odd to believe that all revolves around us; how sad to refuse to accept the gifts we have been given, just as they are. Why do we not realize that we are only travelers, that this is not our ultimate home?

Zen teaches us how to relax our grip. Students come to understand that although they have control over some of their own responses, they are not in charge of everyone else. As this happens they can begin to see each person as he truly is, not as they wish or demand him to be. They also realize that it is an act of violence, not an act of love, to want to change and control another person for their own ends.

As we meditate, we learn to let each moment, each breath and each person be exactly as he is. We let the environment be as it is, the lights as bright or dim, the temperature as hot or cold. We do not control or manipulate anything. This is the great work of *doing* nothing. It is the work of noninterference with the primal wisdom of the universe, with divine harmony, which runs through all things and beings, including ourselves. When we step back and allow this divine harmony (*dharma*) to take over, our entire lives are healed and made pure. When we honor and uphold life as it is given, then inevitably life honors and upholds us.

Rena came to the zendo after losing two important relationships. Devastated, she was convinced she could never hold on to love. She believed everyone would leave her eventually; that was her fate.

When asked why she was here, she told the Zen master, "I can't bear losing even one more person."

"You will lose many," the Zen master said.

Rena gasped.

"Inevitable."

"What can I *do* about it?" Rena shot back.

"Do nothing," the Zen master said.

DO NOTHING

Some people are like mad dogs who bark
at every passing breeze.
—HUANG PO

Do nothing is an elaboration of *don't move*. It is the basis of all Zen teachings. Unfortunately, this instruction has been greatly misunderstood. It does not mean be passive, accept your fate, surrender to helplessness. Just the opposite. *Do nothing* is the most challenging, demanding, revolutionary instruction that can be given. This command is active—

when you sit there, not moving, then *do* nothing. Let go of control. When you are faced with a difficult knot in a relationship, don't squirm and wrestle, don't enter into a struggle, *do* nothing—give up control. Stay centered and immovable in the middle of the storm and see what the conflict is truly about. Let it live out its own life. Let it come and let it go. Don't get picked up and whirled around like a leaf in the wind.

Most of our actions and behavior (especially when they arise from the busy, confused and scattered mind) create more upset, static, complications and unpleasant consequences. Most of our actions are not truly actions, but simply *reactions*. They arise from our conditioning, compulsions and frenzied desires. These are the activities upon which karma is built.

True action is something different. It is clear, spontaneous, purposeful, direct. True action arises from a totally different part of our being.

TRUE ACTION

Do you have the patience to wait until the mud settles?
—ZEN SAYING

In order to arrive at *true action* we must *first do nothing*. This means we must stop doing what we used to do. We must cease our reflexive reactions. We must stop living like Sisyphus, rolling the same rock up the same mountain. We must be able to bear the anxiety, confusion and whatever else arises when we simply stop our usual mode of reacting. We must be willing to be very still and silent so our impulse to react has time to fade out. If we can do this in relationships, many small upsets dissolve naturally. We give them room to come and go. We do not fan the flames by reacting. We do not turn a summer rain into a violent thunderstorm, which can tear apart an entire relationship.

For many individuals, when they stop doing what they are used to doing it feels like a kind of little death. They think that who they are is what they do.

Andrew, whose fiancée had just left him, was told to sit still in the zendo and not move until he heard the bell. As tension mounted and his sensations intensified, he began to feel unbearably restless. First he had to reach out and brush a fly off his arm. Then a few minutes later, he just had to scratch his nose. Andrew vaguely knew he was disturbing others by flailing out in this manner, but he couldn't stand what he was feeling. He had to change and control his environment. He barely realized the effect he was having on others, which is what his fiancée knew all too well.

In relationships the same dynamic takes place. First one thing, then another arrives to cause agitation. We flail out, trying to change or control what we're feeling or change the person who's making us feel this way. We think our comfort is much more important than theirs. Naturally, sooner or later this kind of attitude drives them away.

Andrew wasn't even aware of Jennifer, who was sitting beside him and gritting her teeth each time he moved. He was dimly conscious that nobody else in the zendo was moving, and he did feel a little embarrassed, but he was first, after all, wasn't he?

Everyone wants to be first, most important, the center of the world, and wants his relationships to prove that he is. However, this kind of attitude always backfires, leaving the person depressed and alone. It is crucial to realize that we do not always have to be *first* in relationships. Until we realize that, we are unable to naturally fall in love. Wanting to be first, the best, the center of everything, pushes love far from our doorstep.

When we sit together in the zendo and *do* nothing, when we don't move, we see that all of us have equal importance, that anything that bothers or hurts others, hurts us equally. We also honor others by helping create an environment where all can sit strongly without disturbance and become larger than their passing irritations and complaints.

Jennifer, thirty, an attractive, intelligent graphic designer, finally met the man of her dreams. He was her age exactly, had a wonderful sense of style, was funny, intelligent and able to be close. They had been dating for three months, felt terrific together and she truly wanted it to last. However, she soon noticed that he watched sports too often, spent too much time with his friends, enjoyed taking bicycle tours alone and often tended to be late. Jennifer desperately wanted to control these things about him, change him, whip him into shape. But she had a sinking feeling that, as with her past boyfriends, the effort would be too much, that it either wouldn't work or he would end up resenting her for it. Why did all of her relationships seem to have things wrong like this? Would there ever be someone who was 100 percent *right?*

WHEN WILL IT ALL BE RIGHT?

You can never see anything worse than yourself.
—ESHIN

For Jennifer and others like her, nothing feels right unless it is exactly as they want it to be. They are driven by an intense need to control others, their world, their feelings and especially their romantic relationships, where increased vulnerability, along with fear of rejection and loss, can cause considerable anxiety.

Jennifer was not able to allow her boyfriends to be who they were, to accept their differences or any behavior that did not mirror her values or reflect well upon her. As a result, she felt compelled to change and improve each boyfriend, creating power struggles, tension and ultimately loss in a relationship that could have been satisfying. Soon it became clear, even to Jennifer, that the problem did not lie in the other person, but in her fierce need for power and control.

By now it was easy for Jennifer to see that as she went from one man to another, her efforts never rehabilitated them. She had only so much power and no more. She was confused, however, about how a situation could be altered if she did nothing. Who would be in charge?

At this point Jennifer decided to try Zen practice, and her whole mode of being was turned upside down. One day she was placed next to Andrew, who moved and squirmed relentlessly during the entire sitting. Jennifer did her best not to move despite her desire to lean over, grab Andrew's hands and tie them behind his back. She sat straight and still, allowing herself to experience what was going on. By not moving, she was unable to run away or influence her experience. She had to simply be present to whatever was happening, just as it was. As she sat there, thoughts running, heart racing, she suddenly realized that Andrew was no different from herself. In a crazy way he was showing her how she lived, desperate to control every moment, afraid to take things as they came. Despite herself, Jennifer smiled. By the time the bell rang at the end of the sitting, she actually felt compassion for Andrew, as though he were a lifelong friend.

All our squirming, moving, changing, fixing is simply a defense mechanism that allows us to avoid being with and seeing the truth of who we are—and how we are in relationships. It also prevents us from seeing the other and opening up to love. Love has nothing to do with how the other person is behaving. It has nothing to do with changing him to suit our values and dreams. That is self-centered manipulation. Love enters through a different door.

MUD IS JUST MUD

When he was enlightened he could walk through mud without being upset. He realized mud was just mud.
—DOGEN ZENJI

Many individuals feel their lives have been destroyed by painful relationships and by situations that they could not change or control.

When we walk through something that is distasteful to us, or enter a relationship that is hurtful or not going our way, we ascribe all kinds of interpretations to it. We decide that this unpleasant situation reflects upon ourselves—that we must fight and change it in order to have our dignity back. We decide that someone is our enemy, and move to strengthen our defenses. We believe we are always being rejected and will never love again.

These beliefs and interpretations that we add to the situation are what get us stuck in the mud of our lives. They prevent us from moving on. They leave us feeling soiled and muddied. They make us feel we have been wounded and wronged. They whisper that revenge is needed. We repeat these ideas to ourselves many, many times. When we believe these stories and react to them, we lose touch with what is truly happening now and what is presently available to us. And more than that, we lose touch with the fact that mud is just mud.

Dogen Zenji (a great Zen master) could walk through all kinds of conditions and remain unaffected because he didn't add anything to them. He was right where he was, experiencing everything directly. Mud wasn't bad or defiling. It was just mud. As he passed through it, on his way, he would soon be walking on a field of grass. When grass appeared on his journeys, it wasn't heaven, it was just grass. When grass faded in the autumn, it wasn't because he was being punished, subjected to a harrowing winter. It was just that it was time for grass to fade. After winter, something else would arise.

Most of us cannot walk in this manner through the conditions and events of life. We keep trying to turn mud into pure water. When we encounter a grassy field, we try to keep it green even as we are facing the winter frost. We fear the new terrain that life presents to us instead of simply moving forward into it.

We do precisely the same thing in relationships. We keep dwelling upon one situation, how we've been wronged in it, ruminating about it and refusing to let go. We are upset by the fact that we were not able to control our situation and feel helpless as a result. But what is it that we can truly control? Because we cannot control this unfathomable world, does it mean that we are helpless, or fools? Is there another way we can approach both the beauty and the pain that we feel?

As we engage faithfully in Zen practice, we become more able to realize that mud is just mud. It is not there to debase, distress or stop us. We accept it in our travels, walk through it and simply move on.

WHEN HE COMES WE WELCOME, WHEN HE GOES WE DO NOT PURSUE

This simple instruction is a direct way of turning our lives around. If we truly follow it in all our relationships, we create heaven on earth, no matter who comes or goes. We do not grab on to others, claiming them as our own. We realize where each person came from and where he is going.

We welcome anyone who comes, not with blame, demands or disappointment, but with the understanding that each person is a precious gift, given to us for a certain period of time. When the time comes for that person to depart, we honor his departure and do not pursue—we do not create guilt or blame because he is departing. When others feel the respect and space this gives them, it opens the door for them to be all they can and creates a fertile ground and a safe place for love.

The instruction reminds us to take everything in stride. It

helps us not to move, not to interfere with the natural rhythm of the universe, which inevitably brings what is ours to us, and removes that which is not for us now.

Jennifer had a hard time applying this in her relationships, but as she did, an amazing thing began to happen. First, she began to feel less disturbed by the faults she found in the men in her life. Their so-called faults just became part of a larger picture. She let them be as they were. The men she was with, not feeling so criticized (either verbally or nonverbally), began to relax and show more enjoyable aspects of themselves. Jennifer couldn't believe it.

The power struggles that had informed all her relationships were naturally subsiding. Time together was no longer mainly about who was in charge, but simply about being together for now. A great pressure had been released by both parties. Something new was now possible.

The more we practice, the more we become in touch with the great natural wisdom of the universe and with the process of ongoing change. We become able to find our center and well-being in that which is beyond the passing currents. As we let go of control, not only is great energy restored to us, but we become able to see the root from which real love grows.

Welcoming someone when he comes, not pursuing when he goes, is a manifestation of a life of love. The more we enter this way of life, the more full and joyous we become, not swimming against the tides of life, but becoming able to play in the waves and enjoy the ride thoroughly.

WHO'S IN CHARGE?

Although many profess to believe in God, deep within they believe they live in a random, chaotic universe that they somehow have the power to control. They are the ones who know best, are right, and need to be in charge of others. Not only is this a grandiose delusion (arising in childhood, when the infant feels that it is the center of the world), it is the vivid working of the false self, or ego, that dominates many lives and destroys most relationships. Many spend time in relationships in power struggles, feeling that if they win, they will have gained love. Nothing could be farther from the truth. The more someone tries to control and change you, the more out of control he feels. Entering into a power struggle with him only fuels his sense of powerlessness and achieves nothing for either of you.

The only solution to a situation like this is to realize one's true underpinnings, to become connected to the profound source of support and strength for all life. When this happens, true power and centeredness arises. The connection to the truth of one's being is established, and struggle is a thing of the past. Relationships are then formed on an entirely different basis.

Stepping-Stones to Love
Relinquishing Control

1. WHO ARE YOU CONTROLLING?

For a few moments each day, take time to notice what it is you want to control. Who are you intent on changing? What is it you won't let go away? Spend a few moments with each situation. Then, very gently, ask yourself what would happen if you let this person be just as he is. Realize he doesn't belong to you, but has simply crossed your pathway. (This is true for a mate, parent and child as well.) Do this for a little while each day. See how it feels.

2. STOP MOVING

Take some time to notice the situations or relationships in which you are constantly moving, busy, fixing something and worried about the outcome. What would happen if you stopped all this activity and decided you weren't going to control?

In the middle of the situation or relationship, just don't move. Stop your usual reactive behavior. *Do* nothing. Realize there is a larger wisdom that can harmonize and control. Let the situation or relationship be what it is for now, let it move and change on its own. Become a mountain in the middle of it. Realize it is not necessarily up to you to create the outcome. Who is it up to?

3. ABANDONING POWER STRUGGLES

Realize that power struggles become addictions. They drain joy and energy from relationships, and more than that, they can never be won. If you are in a power struggle in a relationship, let it go. Stop playing the complementary role. Also, do not let another control you. Controlling and being controlled have nothing to do with love.

Focus upon who you are, stay grounded in your own truth. More than that, take time to realize who really is in control. What is the true source of power in relationships? Is there any power greater than love?

4. WHO'S IN CHARGE?

When we begin to let go of controlling, a much larger question appears. The real issue is, who's in charge? Where do change, love and joy come from? At moments when you become less reactive, stop and ask yourself: who's in charge? (Don't push for an answer. When it's ready, an answer may come on its own. Just asking the question is wonderful. It's all that's needed from you.)

5. WALKING THROUGH MUD

Where is the mud that you must walk through in your life? Notice. How do you react to it? What do you tell yourself about it? How do you try to circumvent walking through this mud? (Do you put on blinders, earphones, generate fantasies of all kinds?) What happens when you do?

Now try something different. Just walk through the mud

simply, realizing it's nothing but mud. None of the things you tell yourself about it are the reality of what's going on. Mud is just mud. If you walk through it in this way, it will not be able to stick to you.

6. LETTING HIM COME AND LETTING HIM GO

When someone comes into your life (or day), practice letting him come. Simply welcome the person, letting him be as he is.

When it is time for a person to go away, practice letting him go. Do not turn it into an experience of loss, rejection or abandonment. Realize it has nothing to do with you; it is simply time for him to go.

Do this with yourself as well. Let yourself come and go freely in life, not tying yourself in unnecessary chains.

The Master gives himself up to whatever the moment brings.
—ZEN SAYING

Part Two

ZEN IN ACTION

Chapter 4

KINHIN: WALKING MEDITATION
(taking new steps)

Attentively, watch your step.
—TOREI ZENJI

A BABY HAS NO PROBLEM TAKING NEW STEPS.
When it comes time to walk, although she has not yet found her balance, she arises, stumbles, gets up and tries again. If she gets hurt, she cries for a moment, wipes herself off and moves on. No one walks without first falling down. No one falls down without momentarily getting hurt. We fall down, get up, go on, get lost, get found and then get lost again.

The same is true in relationships. We do not necessarily have our balance as we begin. We may need a great deal of exploration to find out who we are, who the other is and how to meet one another's needs. It can be said that no greater bravery is required than the bravery it takes to move forward in love.

Relationships by their very nature can become chaotic. Maintaining balance and clarity are much harder in the throes of a loving relationship, in which needs and feelings are intensified and loyalties can become divided. Many people in situations like this feel as though they are walking on a tightrope.

In life we are constantly accosted by endless stimuli, people wanting different things from us, choices that must be made on the spot. We must often take action without taking time to consider the consequences. We learn to list our priorities and proportion our time in order to create a balanced life and tend to the various parts of our selves. Although we follow the schedule we have set out, we don't necessarily achieve a sense of inner balance as well. Conflicts can still rage within. These inner conflicts are not always resolved by rational planning, or by efforts to convince ourselves of what the right next move may be. In fact, the more we think about what to do, the wobblier we can become.

As we undertake Zen practice our sense of rhythm and timing in relationships becomes fine-tuned. We naturally know when it's time to take action and when it's time to be still. We are released from both procrastination and impulsive behavior that is not based upon what is real, or what is needed at the moment. In touch with our own innate balance, our relationships become balanced as well.

WHEN IT'S TIME TO WALK, WALK: A ZENDO LESSON

Walk to the left, walk to the right, but above all, don't wobble.
—ZEN SAYING

Our body can teach us all we need to know. First our body must come into balance, then the very manner in which we walk upon the earth will show us the next step to take.

In Zen practice, sooner or later each sitting is ended by the sound of a bell. This bell indicates it is time to rise from the cushion and prepare to walk. This ceremonial walking between periods of zazen is known as *kinhin*. This is not a casual walk or break, but walking meditation. The concentration and attentiveness developed on the cushion during zazen is now extended into action.

During kinhin, students are instructed to keep their backs straight, hands folded together under the breastbone, heads straight and eyes to the floor. When kinhin begins, one student walks behind another, paying attention to the bottom of his own feet. It is easy to maintain focus and balance when one sits on the cushion. It is another matter to be focused and centered when one gets up into activity.

Some have no difficulty sitting in zazen. In fact, they love it, are thrilled to sit down and relinquish the turmoil that has invaded their lives. They resent the sound of the bell at the end of each sitting, which calls them back into activity. It's difficult for them to go from the precious silence into motion again. However, no matter how deep or lovely the sitting has been, when the bell rings out, that sitting is over. All in the zendo have to get up and move. We often become attached to one state, one activity or one relationship and do not want to let it be over and move on to what is next. In the same manner, some individuals become unable to switch smoothly and naturally from one phase of life to the next.

"When it comes time to get up, get up," the instructor will say. "When the time comes to move, no matter what we feel like, we move."

Some students get up begrudgingly, irritated.

The instructor will neither notice nor comment upon their mood. "Just watch every step attentively," he'll say.

EVERYONE THINKS HE KNOWS WHAT HE NEEDS

Everyone always thinks he knows what he needs when he comes to the zendo—just as he thinks he knows why he enters this relationship or that one. Everyone thinks he knows what must happen to make him content. (Of course, if these thoughts were accurate, by now the whole world would be content.) However, there are many awakenings and surprises in store—both at the zendo and in relationships. It's better to become a little humble and realize that in both cases, there's a lot to learn.

We are so eager to jump to superficial conclusions based upon initial appearances. If we walk slowly in a line, we think that is all we are doing. If we make lists of what's important, we think we are solving problems. If some feeling of attachment arises, we think we are in love.

Kinhin is not about walking around in a line. It teaches us to stay alert, focused and mindful when we are in action, when we are confronted by stimuli, as when we are sitting in silence. It teaches us to take appropriate action, whether or not we want to, right now.

How many relationships have been lost or have faltered because a partner cannot take the next appropriate step. Some cannot say, "I love you," or commit to making the relationship deeper. Others are unable to listen fully or respond to their partner's needs. How many end up stuck, sitting still in their relationship, though the bell has rung out many times? So many refuse to hear the sound of the bell in their relationships, the many warnings and indications that an aspect is over and it is time to go to the next phase. (Of course this is true not only in relationships, but in all aspects of our lives.) In the zendo, however, when the bell rings out, we cannot miss it. We have no choice.

When we apply this principle to our relationships as well, we learn to move on when the time comes, and to decrease our attachment to a person or situation that is no longer appropriate for us. Zen shows us that we do not have to cling to where we are, or try to return to a past situation. Instead we readily enter the next activity or experience that is waiting for us. Similarly, if it is time to move forward in the relation-ship—to move in together or become engaged—we are able to take those steps as well, stay with our present actions, not falter, or become derailed by fears of the future or thoughts of what the consequences may bring. Fear of the future and longing for the past are major factors that impede appropri-ate action. As we become able to take action in the present, both of those factors lose power over our lives.

MOVING ON: LIVING IN THE PRESENT

If we could just follow this instruction—just to be able to move on when it's time to move on—our lives would fall into perfect balance. We'd be cured of procrastination and ob-session and forced to get up and out (whether or not we want to), enter the flow of life, become comfortable with all kinds of activities, do what's needed *when* it's needed and maintain our balance and inner center throughout it all.

Timing is of the essence in relationships, just as it is in all aspects of our lives. We must have the presence of mind, balance and intuitive connection to others to know what to do when. We must know instinctively what is needed and wanted, what the timing dictates—when to take a few steps closer, and when to back away. Without this inner knowing-ness, we either crowd others, or leave them feeling empty and cold. So many people walk around in circles, never knowing when to stop and make contact.

Tom went to one singles party after another, searching for someone to love. When he walked in the door he felt fantastic. There were so many beautiful women to choose from. He felt he could have anyone.

Tom would enter, go to the bar, get a drink to bolster his spirits, then start to circle the room. Because he was good-looking, he attracted attention, and initially many women looked over, interested. Tom would glance back at them briefly and, with a drink in his hand, keep roaming, checking out the whole scene.

"I didn't want to miss a thing. I was checking them all out," Tom explained to his disheartened therapist. "You never know who's around the corner. I wasn't ready to stop somewhere and talk. Who knows what would happen then? I could get stuck with someone all night long."

Tom did not want to stop and sit down. He kept circling around the edges of the party, checking everyone out. Before he knew it, the party was ending and once again, Tom was going home alone. He hadn't known when to stop and walk over to someone. He could never tell the right time to say hello.

Tom desperately needed to learn how to stop and be still for a time, get up when the bell rang and walk, focusing upon nothing but the next step. When his attention was scattered he could not focus upon anything or anyone. Tom needed to feel the floor under his feet when he walked, not to wander around pointlessly, following the fantasies in his head. He had to allow another part of himself to take over and learn to move in accordance with his natural balance. Tom was always astonished when the evening was over and he hadn't "hooked up" with anyone.

Usually we do not fully realize the beginning and end of anything. One activity, one relationship easily flows into the next. But it is also impossible to be truly available for a new relationship, to be ready and present, unless we realize that the one before it is over—or has significantly changed its form. Someone who was once a lover may now be a good friend. Someone we heard from continually may now rarely call at all. Someone who was a passing acquaintance may have developed other feelings. How can we act appropriately in each situation if we don't know where we are? So many are haunted by the ghosts of past relationships that they are not present for what is available now.

WHAT IS NEEDED NOW

When one moment, one action or one person blends into another, it is difficult to realize where we are now and what is presently called for. It is hard to know when to come or when to go. So many people live in the past, mulling over and dreaming about what happened before, that they have no inner space or energy to meet the person who is here right now, in front of their eyes.

Tom had to be able to stop his roaming, no matter what he was feeling, go up to someone (anyone at all), and greet her. He had to stay with her for a while, find out about her and talk to her. Tom needed to take appropriate action, no matter how he felt. By connecting with even one individual, he would confront the delusions that ran him, telling him no one was right for him, that the perfect person hadn't arrived yet. His job was not to search for the perfect person, but simply to stop and be with someone for a while, to make friends, give up the crazy game he was playing. Standing still with one person, looking at her, talking and listening, would be a form of Zen practice for Tom. As he did it consistently, little by little, his restlessness would subside and he would be able to become present to what was really going on and what was available.

ATTENTIVELY, WATCH YOUR STEP

A Zen master was asked about the essence of Zen training.

"Attention," he said.
"What else?" asked the student.
"Attention. Attention. Attention," came the reply.

It is of the utmost importance to learn how to defuse the illusions, fears and confusion that besiege us in all that we do. "Attentively, watch your step" is a fundamental lesson of Zen. Take charge of your attention. Place it right here, on this very step, this precise action. Do not allow the inner or outer chaos to influence what you do.

Usually when we are involved in activity, when we encounter new stimuli or change, different people or situations that are challenging, our attention disperses. We become intoxicated by all that is going on. Adrenaline starts pumping, fantasies, reactions, thoughts and images flood our being. The body goes on high alert. It is easy to get thrown off balance, to feel pulled in many directions and lose our sense of where we are. It is also easy to become confused about what to do or where to go.

By training the body, we also train the mind. By attending to the body, we attend to our entire life. The body will show us where our mind is. A wobbling body is a manifestation of a wobbling mind. A stagnant body is a manifestation of a mind that is stuck, holding on.

Lisa, thirty-eight, a successful banker who is divorced with two children, finally met someone new that she liked. The relationship came out of the blue and swept her off her feet. While she used to leave work long after everyone else, she now found herself leaving at five sharp to get in an early dinner—and sometimes a movie—with her new boyfriend. While she used to spend Saturday nights watching movies with the kids, she now found herself leaving the house by six for a night out on the town. Time with the kids became harder to manage, but at the same time she didn't want to give up this relationship, which made her feel whole again.

As the demands upon her both at the office and at home

increased, the conflict began to take its toll on both Lisa and her boyfriend. She began to feel stretched so thin that any little irritation with him became blown out of proportion. She constantly felt as though she had to make a choice between him and the rest of her life.

When Lisa finally came to Zen practice she did not realize that to "attentively watch each step" could solve her problems of balancing family, work and love life. It was as simple as that. (Sometimes too simple is difficult. We yearn for the complications and difficulties we are accustomed to. It can take a while to be weaned off the taste for chaos and learn to thoroughly enjoy walking attentively, feeling every step.)

"Just pay careful attention to every step," Lisa was instructed as she wobbled along on the line.

At first she couldn't do it. Her attention, and thus her body, was wavering back and forth. As Lisa struggled to only pay attention to the bottom of her feet while moving, to every single step, she realized how hard it was for her to fully be where she was. This was also true in relationships, where she was constantly wondering about what would happen next, how the other felt about her, how larger issues would be resolved. Her obsession with future planning prevented her from being right here. The place the two of them were in right now, the step they were presently taking, seemed insignificant compared to the huge problems she felt the future held. By paying attention to this very step, to her actual life at this moment, Lisa felt she was abandoning the rest of her world. As a result she had become drained and torn, completely losing the center of her own being. Naturally, this impacted her ability to fall, and stay, in love.

But as her practice of kinhin continued and Lisa learned how to move from one activity to the next and not be pulled back by random feelings, she began to find room for different activities, people and needs. She could put one mode of being aside and enter another. When she left the office, she left it behind her and made room for different parts of herself to be expressed.

Lisa learned that we can never truly be there for another unless we are fully with ourselves. This does not mean being selfish or self-absorbed; it means knowing who and where we are now, the feel of our feet on the floor. It means being in touch with the core of one's being, one's own intuitive self. Without having that connection, it is easy to become prey for everything that approaches. This is no better than living like a leaf blown about in the wind.

Zazen practice shows us how to regain our center. It vigorously pulls our mind and attention back from the endless phenomena that claim it moment by moment, and places it squarely in the center of ourselves.

By paying attention to this very moment, to exactly what we are doing as we do it, we become part of the rest of the world. We become oriented, balanced and clear. We know where we are when we are there. We also learn where we aren't and how we got from here to there.

As we dash through life, not taking a second to experience where we are, we lose not only balance, but access to the enormous wisdom that is always available when our minds and hearts are collected. When we are not collected, when there's nobody home, there's room for all kinds of people to enter our world and all kinds of events to happen to us before we can realize what's going on.

RETURN TO YOUR ROOT

The heart and fruit of all Zen practice is to return to your own root. Before you *do* anything, or choose any destination, you must know where you are coming from. Return to your root first and all will be clear. Don't focus entirely on your problem. This person, situation or problem is not outside you. It has been brought to you so that you might grow. Finding out what the person or situation needs from you, and what you need as well, can be a fascinating journey. As you return to your root, the truth of the matter becomes very clear.

When we return to our root we understand the different ways in which we love different people. Not everyone is suitable to be our mate. However, if we feel trapped in an intimate relationship with someone who feels inappropriate for that role, it is often impossible to leave the relationship until we have learned how to love and accept who they are. We must become able to forgive, honor and acknowledge the goodness they have to give. Some say that each person who comes into our lives comes to give and receive a blessing. Once this is accomplished, their appropriate place in our lives is easy to find.

Cara came to the zendo because she found herself married to a man she did not love. "I never loved him," she exclaimed disconsolately. "I loved someone else. My boyfriend and I had a huge fight one night and then I met my husband on the rebound. A momentum took over, like a stream I couldn't stop. Before I knew it I woke up one morning, married. When I look at him I don't feel any love. I want to leave him, but I'm scared. Still, scared or not, I can't bear living my whole life without feeling love."

Like everyone else, Cara received her instructions—to sit on the cushion, follow her breath, not to move, and to get up when the bell rang for kinhin. Because she was somewhat desperate, she didn't object to anything.

"Fine," she said. "I'll do it gladly. And will this help me leave my husband?"

"Who knows?" said the instructor.

"That's not really good enough," Cara replied. "If I do all of this will I be able to leave him?"

We are usually pleased to do something if it fits into our preconceived ideas about the outcome. We walk to get somewhere rather than walk to feel each step on the ground. We need motivation for taking action, rather than taking action for its own sake and letting the action itself lead us to the correct destination.

"Before you leave him," replied the instructor, "stop leaving yourself."

That stopped Cara. Something has to stop us before we are willing to pay attention, to try a new way. Cara was being told to return to her root.

Cara had become so lost in her life she had no idea anymore where home base was. She believed her inability to be in love with her husband had to do with who he was. He seemed like a stranger to her in the mornings, lying there at her side.

Until we truly know ourselves, all others are strangers to us. Until we are able to understand how we got from here to there, to find the root that plants us, it is difficult to maintain a life of love. Sometimes, due to karma or circumstances beyond our control, we find ourselves in a relationship or a situation that we have no idea how we got into, or how to relate to. We feel helpless and lonely, not knowing what to do.

As Cara practiced she began to notice new aspects of her husband. He did not seem so foreign and strange. The closer she became to herself, the more she could include him. One morning she abruptly realized his many kindnesses to her. She sat at the breakfast table and began to cry. He came over and put his hand on her shoulder.

"It takes time," he said softly.

Cara was completely taken aback.

Perhaps it is Cara's *koan*, an insoluble problem that we must nevertheless solve (we will talk of koans later in another chapter), to be with this unexpected husband so she can truly learn how to fall in love (or that she can truly learn to leave). The first step for her is to realize that falling in love has little to do with someone else. It has everything to do with her own state of mind, what she brings to the situation and how she perceives both of them.

Every being on earth is lovable. If we are not able to love them it is simply because there are clouds over our eyes. These clouds can drift away anytime we want them to.

Zen practice is about returning to the root, to our original selves, the selves we were before we got caught by phenomena. This root is with us all the time. It has never been lost. It is the ability to be hopeful, trusting, open, forgiving and loving, to see and honor the best in everyone and everything.

> When we return to the root we gain the meaning,
> When we chase branches, we lose the substance.
> —SOSAN GANCHI ZENJI, *ON BELIEVING IN MIND*

Stepping-Stones to Love Moving On

1. ONE STEP AT A TIME

As soon as you get up in the morning, become aware of the steps you take. Feel the floor under your feet. Stand tall. Take a few moments to be with each step you take. If you want to rush around as usual, just take note of that and continue being aware of each step you take. As you do this, you can also ask yourself lightly, where am I right now? Where am I going? Be aware of going from here to there. Be aware when time comes to a standstill.

2. THE CENTER OF THE CIRCLE

Some of us feel that we are going in circles, being pulled from one activity (relationship, problem or demands) to the next. See where you go in circles. Notice the forces pulling you. (Although they seem outside of you, on a deeper level they are also within. You are giving acquiescence to them.) Now, stop going around and place yourself in the center of the circle. (Do this in any way that feels right to you.) Let the circle rotate around you and realize that you are the hub of the wheel. Do this in your relationships as well, especially one that seems to be spinning out of control.

3. GETTING LOST AND GETTING FOUND

Stop and notice the areas in your life in which you feel lost, or where you feel you have gone astray. Take a moment to acknowledge that this is part of the human condition and doesn't mean there's something wrong with you. Blame isn't necessary. Give yourself kindness and respect anyhow. It's great to realize that you've gotten lost. The first step in getting found is to realize that you've lost your way. Also, realize if you knew how to get back to home base, you would have by now.

At this moment, see if you are willing to try a different

way of getting found. See if you are willing to just fully be where you are, every step of the way. Practice this a little bit each day and notice what happens. Even practice being with things you don't like or that aren't necessarily making you happy. Practice this with your relationships. Don't try to decide what's going to happen next, or how you're going to get in deeper or get out, just completely take whatever step you're taking now. (If you like keeping a journal, then day by day, write down what happens.) You can also do this with a partner, and after a bit of time share what is going on.

Getting lost and found is a lifelong process. It's actually beautiful and interesting. We may think we're lost, but if we look with a larger eye, what is our true destination anyhow?

4. INCLUDING ALL PARTS OF YOURSELF

Where do you find it hard to move on? Where do you feel unable to balance the demands made of you? Take a moment and see what is keeping you stuck. What are you holding on to? (What person, idea, belief or fear?) What will happen if you let go and move on to what is next? (This can apply to one person, one activity or one phase of life.)

Take a moment to recognize and honor the place that you have been. Honor the activity, person or situation you are having trouble leaving. Realize that by moving onward and including more you are not abandoning anything, but simply providing a larger context for your life. Spend some time doing this. Spend some time honoring the place and the person.

5. RETURN TO THE ROOT

This is an exercise we will do throughout the rest of the book. As your practice continues, the root grows deeper and more firm.

Notice: Where do you feel that the root in your life is now? What most deeply connects you to yourself and to all of life? What do you trust and have faith in? Be simple, honest and clear with yourself in answering these questions. No one has to know your answers. Do not fear answering in ways that are unexpected, or that change from day to day. This is time for honest exploration.

Some of us have roots that do not connect us to that which is nourishing or beneficial for our lives. Rather than just yank up these kinds of roots, it is preferable to first take a good look at them and slowly replace them with new roots that will connect to that which brings true life and love.

6. TAKE A NEW STEP

Now that you begin to have a sense of what your roots are, perhaps you can venture to take a new step today—just one. Spend a few moments realizing where you have stopped venturing and what new step you might want or need to take. Then take it. Just one step in a new direction—not two. Take that one step bravely and fully. Tomorrow you can take another one. You may take this step either in your personal life or in a relationship. The important point here is just to get used to taking new steps every day. No matter what you are thinking and feeling, step by step, include something new. Move on to the next phase in your life. Your steps will show you how to go.

> Travelers,
> there is no path.
> Paths are made by walking.
> —Antonio Machado

Chapter 5

CLEANING HOUSE
(emptying yourself)

Empty-handed he comes, empty-handed he goes.
—KIDO, IN *ZEN FLESH, ZEN BONES*

WE ALL CHERISH OUR BEAUTIFUL POSSESSIONS, attainments and memories, and enjoy the warmth they provide. While these are positive supports in our lives, it is also important to learn how not to cling to what we have accumulated, to be able to let go, clean house and make room for new experiences and gifts to arise.

This is true as well in our relationships. All of us come to new relationships filled to the brim with memories, fears, ideas, beliefs and pictures of how we want things to go. However, as soon as things don't go our way, the moment we feel slighted, misunderstood or unwanted, alarms start to sound. We then begin withdrawing, fighting or rejecting the person. Most of us are time bombs waiting to go off—especially in love relationships, where our hearts and sense of value are on the line. How is it then ever possible to be available to someone new? How can we decrease our defensiveness and innate expectation of harm?

Some say that in fact it is good to be on the alert, to build appropriate defenses, sift out the good from the bad. They say it is foolish to be wide open, fundamentally trusting and joyfully in love. The best we can do is learn how to tolerate the fluctuations that occur in relationships. Being open and trusting is for children, those who aren't realistic and haven't yet experienced the sorrows love can bring. But love does not bring sorrow. The baggage we carry, the garbage we accumulate and hold on to, is the cause of our suffering. That and nothing else.

Many of us who have not come to terms with relationships also happen to live in homes that are filled to the brim, with hardly an inch left to move. We have accumulated endless possessions and memories and often find these owning us and running our lives, instead of the other way around. This clutter prevents change and freedom of movement in both our inner and outer worlds. We can't possibly love, trust and be present when we are filled with clutter and confusion.

CLEANING OUR LIVES OUT:
A ZENDO LESSON

When we learn to clean our house and lives thoroughly, to remove clutter and let go of the past, space arises for our relationships to breathe freely and for love to appear.

In the zendo, students take turns at different jobs that are essential to the running of a zendo. Zendos are always beautifully cared for and immaculate. They are also empty, containing only that which is absolutely needed and used at the present time. Nothing extra is left over and nothing is kept lying around.

In many zendos, cleaning requires the student get down on her hands and knees, hold a damp cloth and, inch by inch, push it along the floor. This is not casual cleaning, but like kinhin done carefully and precisely, in silence, with the greatest mindfulness. The student is always directly connected with the activity she is doing. As she does it with great concentration she, the rag, the floor and the zendo become one. By cleaning in this manner, many things are accomplished, not the least of which is that she makes the zendo her own.

Cleaning duties range from sweeping the grounds to cleaning the toilets. Everyone takes a turn at all assignments. No one is too good or important to clean the toilet. In fact, the toilet isn't considered less important than the altar, just as one person isn't considered more important than anyone else. In the zendo every moment and aspect of life is revered and cared for.

OPENING TO THE CHILDLIKE MIND

The great man is he who does not lose his childlike heart.
—MENICUS

As we clean our spaces and also our hearts and minds we become supple, light and trusting, and a childlike quality develops within us. We are filled with freshness and wonder. Relationships become an adventure because we are not weighed down by residue from the past. We are ready for new encounters and to be truly available for love. This condition may also be called *the childlike mind*.

There is a huge difference between a *childish* mind and a *childlike* mind. Many of us remain "childish" our whole lives. We do not mature and ripen, but stay fixated upon wishes we had when we were young. Although we may have graduated college, in our love relationships we are still in kindergarten. When we are childish we want to always be the center of attention and grab all the goodies for ourselves. We don't know how to give and take or make room for someone else. We live a life of self-absorption, wanting only what suits ourselves.

The *childlike* mind is different. It is the original mind we were born with before social conditioning and personal experience affected us. The childlike mind is open, natural and expectant. It finds beauty in life and adventure and does not expect to harm or be harmed. It plays naturally, loves to give and receive. This childlike mind is a mind without clutter. It is not carrying around years of wounds. The childlike mind is Zen mind: open, free, eager to delight and enjoy. The childlike mind itself is a manifestation of a life of love.

We have detoured from the simple road to falling in love because we have neglected to sufficiently appreciate and acknowledge the power, wisdom and essential goodness of the childlike, or original, mind. Without discovering and befriending this part of ourselves, we can wander in and out of all kinds of relationships, but true love will not take hold; instead, we will live with drab compromises. Though burying true delight is considered mature by the "reasonable" world, deep within we know life has so much more to offer and we are actually selling ourselves short.

CLEAN YOUR HOUSE THOROUGHLY

In Zen practice the sparseness and cleanliness of the room we sit in or live in naturally affects our state of mind. It also reflects what is going on inside us and is a manifestation of it. The more we learn to clean our spaces, remove that which is no longer needed, the sooner our hearts can become open to experiencing something new. Analyzing our psychological patterns may not do as much as learning how to clean the floor until it absolutely shines.

Soen Roshi, a great modern-day Zen master, said, "In Zen practice, to find the beauty of our home we do not add more furniture or decorations, but remove all that which is unnecessary so the original beauty can manifest." In most places, the beauty of a room is judged by what is placed in it—the furniture, artwork, artifacts. In Zen, the beauty and aliveness of a room is judged by what is taken out. A clear, empty space reveals the room's essential beauty. When we are not distracted by endless bric-a-brac, we can finally truly see, appreciate and relate to the original space we are in; we can truly see the one flower that is placed on the altar in a simple vase.

In the same way, each person is one flower, placed in our path. In order to fully see, appreciate and relate to this person, we cannot be distracted by the endless clutter and bric-a-brac in our minds, by our thoughts, memories and expectations. We must first empty ourselves. Otherwise we never see the flower or the person before us.

GROWING FLOWERS
OUT OF THE MUD

It is said that the lotus flower, which is most beautiful, grows from the mud. Both the mud and the lotus flower are needed. The mud, the dirt and garbage of our lives (and the lives of others), is not something to be rejected, is not to be considered bad or objectionable. When we clean, we learn to dig our hands into it, knowing this mud is necessary in order for the flower of our lives to grow. The difficulties we've faced, our errors and sorrows, are simply fertilizer. Rather than consider ourselves and our errors bad, stupid or sinful, we turn our suffering into excellent compost.

"How is cleaning the floor going to help me forget how my boyfriend cheated?" a student wanted to know.

"Just clean and you'll find out. But clean thoroughly," came the answer.

The student was reluctant to get down on her hands and knees and clean. She usually hired others to do this for her. But no one else can clean the messes that we've made in our own lives and relationships. We have to be willing to get in there, without hating the garbage, without blaming ourselves or the other, and simply clean.

Finally, the student gingerly got down on her knees and gently pushed the cloth back and forth. The floor didn't look much different than before she started. This was only token cleaning, and she knew it. Out of the corner of her eye she saw another woman cleaning with her entire mind focused on what she was doing, rubbing the floor vigorously. The student felt ashamed. She pressed the rag a little harder and more shame and sorrow arose. Not only was she cleaning the floor, the floor was cleaning her. It was scouring the inside of her heart.

As we clean our outside environment, just as when we sit on the cushion, many thoughts arise in our minds. We do not have to wrestle with each memory as it arises. We simply clean it out and let it out and let it go. Before we know it, it becomes fertilizer for new growth.

DOING WHAT NEEDS TO BE DONE

In the zendo, cleaning is a communal effort that serves an important purpose. Not only does it extend the student's practice into action but, practically speaking, it takes care of what needs to be done. When we focus constantly upon what needs to be done—and do it—we have less time to dwell upon the ways in which we have been wronged. Rather than focus upon the past, we are focusing upon what life requires of us now. This practice of staying present and cleaning and removing that which is no longer needed, makes room for the new and allows the one flower on the altar to shine through. It also allows the flower of our lives to bloom.

The same approach must also be applied to relationships—to keep our mind focused upon what is happening right now, to take care of what is needed when it is needed and to create a clear, open space to be in. When we do this the past will inevitably resolve itself and space will be created for something new.

When trouble arises, keep your mind focused upon what is happening right now—don't bring up the past and decide that the same thing is happening all over again. Take care of what is needed in relationships when it is needed; do not let small resentments and grudges build up out of control. Communicate them as soon as they arise. If something needs to be handled, handle it right now. There is a wonderful Zen saying, "Leave no traces." This means do not leave things incomplete between you and another. Don't leave little messes around. Small lies and secrets build huge barriers. Keep the space between the two of you clean and fresh, and that which is healthy and loving will arise all by itself.

PURIFICATION

Tanzan and Ekido, two monks, were once traveling together down a muddy road. A heavy rain was still falling. Coming around a bend, they met a lovely girl in a silk kimono and sash, unable to cross at the intersection.

"Come on, girl," said Tanzan at once. Lifting her in his arms, he carried her over the mud.

Ekido did not speak again until that night when they reached a lodging temple. Then he no longer could restrain himself. "We monks don't go near females," he told Tanzan, "especially not young and lovely ones. It is dangerous. Why did you do that?"

"I left the girl there," said Tanzan.

"Are you still carrying her?"

—FROM *ZEN FLESH, ZEN BONES*,
COMPILED BY PAUL REPS AND NYOGEN SENZAKI

As we clean thoroughly, we learn how to put down what we are carrying. This is also called purification.

Some wonder why their lives are difficult and why most of their relationships cause them pain. They may not be able to find a partner, or if they do, the person leaves or is cruel or unstable. But it is possible to view relationships as a source of purification. Rather than reject difficult, painful situations, another way to look at them is that they have come to teach us many lessons. The way in which we receive these relationships and respond to them can cleanse us and set a new course of action. Relationships can be considered a great opportunity for growth. We can learn an entirely new way of responding to them.

In difficult situations, people are always the tempted to dwell upon anger, hatred and revenge. We can lash out, we can hurt back. From the Zen point of view, this is a grave mistake. Shantideva, a great Tibetan teacher, advises: "When someone I have loved and cared for harms and abuses me, may I regard him as a great sacred friend."

This means that these people have come to help to purify us from hard karma (old thoughts, deeds and actions that are now bearing fruit). They teach us patience, forbearance and the ability to grow spiritually. They've given us an opportunity to resist giving in to anger and revenge and to allow our karma to be purified, and to realize that somehow, somewhere, we have created seeds to permit this situation to occur.

HEALING FROM BETRAYAL

Julie, twenty-four, a recent college graduate who worked as an assistant in an advertising firm, had been through two long-term relationships. In both of these she caught her boyfriend cheating after their having been together for two years. Now in a new relationship, she can't help suspecting her new boyfriend, thinking in the back of her mind that it will happen again. Julie finds herself chastising him for looking at other women, sometimes even when he's not. She knows she's crowding him, and that it's straining their relationship. How can she learn to trust in relationships? How can she escape the harrowing memories that will not leave her alone?

Julie is holding on to memories of the past, unable to either release or integrate them. As a result she has developed both catastrophic expectations about what is going to happen and a lack of confidence in her ability to deal with it when it does. She cannot trust, as she is convinced that her past experiences must repeat themselves. This stimulates both possessiveness and suspiciousness, which not only pushes each new boyfriend away, but also contributes to making her worst fears come true. When we deeply expect and dwell upon something, we are actually causing it to happen, drawing it to ourselves.

Julie presently has no access to her childlike, trusting mind. It is still there, just covered up and crowded out by all she is holding on to.

When Julie finally arrives at the zendo, although she tries to tell others how her boyfriend cheated on her, people don't seem interested. Instead, when work time comes, she is simply instructed on how to completely clean the zendo. The problem isn't with what happened to her, but with all the clutter she's been holding on to. What she needs to do is start to clean.

Before she began Zen practice, all Julie could see about men were the images of her past boyfriends. She projected their failings upon everyone else and never had a chance to see the real person before her now. Once we have cleaned out and discarded that which has hurt us, we do not see reflections of it in the outside world. The more Julie practiced, the dimmer her memory of what happened became. As the painful memories faded, Julie developed the emotional space to attract someone new into her life. She also developed the ability to see the new person through fresh eyes, not punish him for the past, but allow something different to happen.

With our body we clean our surroundings; in our relationships we do not give in to anger or greed, and with our words we say the following:

> All the evil karma ever committed by me since of old
> On account of my beginningless greed, anger and folly
> Born of my body, mouth and thought
> I now confess and purify them all.

This radical statement helps us take responsibility for what is going on in our lives. It is impossible to live a life of love if we consider ourselves the hapless victim of circumstance. When we identify ourselves as a victim and live life in that way, we attract victimizers. When we realize that knowingly, or unknowingly, we may have brought these conditions to pass, we begin the beautiful work of purification. We become conscious of our own beginningless greed, anger and delusions, and realize that it is now time to let these feelings subside.

MIND WEEDS

Mind weeds are the tangles and knots that grow in our minds. They are the fears, negativities and false imaginings that can grow wild if not pulled out. These are the thoughts that grip us, throw dark clouds over everything and sabotage what we have been doing. Mind weeds will strangle the growth in your life unless you know how to pull them out quickly.

As we live now, our rational mind has taken over most functions that are better served by other parts of our selves. By paying attention only to our rational minds, we have placed our trust in only a fraction of who we are and what is truly available to us. Despite the rational mind's usefulness in many ways, one thing it cannot stop doing is creating clutter of all kinds.

Zen practice corrects this. It shows us how to achieve clarity by removing the weeds that strangle our lives. These weeds arise from both within ourselves and without. When we are in the process of removing them, we don't pay attention to where they arise from, or how this problem interacts with that. We don't analyze or rhapsodize about them. We simply recognize a weed as a weed and directly pull it out.

Mark arrived at the zendo weighed down by inexpressible guilt. He had tried hard in therapy, but he still felt bad about who he was. Whatever happened, he blamed himself. When the women he cared for left him, his self-disgust deepened. They were perfect, he thought, and he was a mess who couldn't hold on to anyone. No matter how much he tried to reason the matter out rationally, he always ended up in the same spot.

Mark's feeling of unbearable guilt and Julie's experience with her former boyfriends are mind weeds that were strangling any chance of new love. The more Mark and Julie dwelt upon them, the larger they grew.

At first Julie was afraid to just "let go" of the memory of her boyfriends' infidelities. Letting it go made her feel foolish and vulnerable, as though she would then be leaving herself open to the same thing happening again. She held on to these memories as a warning, reminding her not to be trusting again.

Mark had the same notion. The guiltier he felt, the more he punished himself, and the less he thought the chances were that he would do something awful. A very strange paradox exists in this notion. We hold on to memories or painful emotions, thinking that if we do not discard or forget them, we will have learned something from them, and the terrible event won't recur.

Strangely enough though, the opposite often takes place. The more we remember something, the more we dwell upon it, fight it or resist it, the more we draw it into our lives. *What we pay attention to expands. What we pay attention to we become.* Why pay attention to the negativities that appear in our lives; why not simply clean them out? As we always keep the memory of how we have been wronged foremost in our minds it creates obstacles that prevent the natural cleansing and resolution that life can do on its own. By dwelling upon our problem we are actually blocking healing and renewal.

NATURAL CLEANSING

When we let go of these mind weeds, the painful incidents and memories, we are not discarding warnings or wisdom. We are simply allowing the original mind to release the painful situation. Deep within we know how to handle all things. Deep within real wisdom is able to take this memory, remove the toxicity from it and retain whatever is valuable for us. This is another facet of purification. Just as we wash our hands, face, teeth and hair daily, we must cleanse and pull up our mind weeds. Our original mind then knows how to use what has happened to us to fertilize new, healthy growth.

Otherwise, we live a life of revenge or shame, on alert for trouble and danger, always expecting harm and preparing to retaliate. In other words, we are living one step away from hell. This is why relationships are considered painful. It is not relationships, of course, that are intrinsically painful, but our choice to live in bitterness, fear and resentment, mentally grasping onto all that was painful, without letting go.

GOOD AND BAD—AWAY WITH IT ONCE AND FOR ALL

Gain and loss, right and wrong—away with them
once and for all.
—Sosan Ganchi Zenji, *On Believing in Mind*

This statement has been greatly misunderstood. Some think it means doing away with morality, with distinguishing between right and wrong. Nothing could be further from the truth.

The statement is an instruction to the mind that judges, blames and condemns everything that comes into its path. It is a reminder to use our childlike mind and know that everybody is both "good and bad," and has moments of clarity and moments of confusion. A person who may have done something very "bad" is also capable of great "good." When we see and accept the entire person, forgiveness and renewal are a step away.

What we are actually describing is the process of forgiveness. When you make forgiveness a daily practice, your life becomes saturated with goodness. This is goodness not opposed to "badness," but the goodness of living life as it is. This is one step away from heaven. Your original mind knows how to get you there.

Vimilakirti was a great lay teacher of Zen. One time he was sick. Several monks were told by their master to go visit him. As he was known for his great wisdom and dauntlessness, the monks were somewhat afraid. Nevertheless they traveled to his side.

When they arrived, they asked Vimilakirti why he was sick.

He replied, "I am sick because all beings are sick."

If there was even one person suffering, scared or wounded, Vimilakirti felt it as well. By not overlooking anything—not a spot or a person—we slowly polish the texture of our lives. By taking responsibility for our own responses rather than focusing upon the shortcomings of others, forgiveness and compassion arise naturally. We then do not project our own failings upon others, or reject them for what we cannot accept in ourselves. By accepting the total range of human experience, we do not fixate upon one aspect of a person, making it the whole story, preventing it from giving way to something else. In this way we create the space for ourselves and others to become new day by day. When our lens of perception has been cleansed, the world is seen through new eyes. At this point, it is almost impossible to dwell upon the failings and errors of those we meet. Then, whoever we meet, wherever we go, becomes an avenue through which we become free to love.

When you are able to see the entire person before you and accept both the beautiful and painful elements, you will not be fixated on darkness and fear, but on the fullness and freshness of all that is. Rather than cling to painful memories, you will be open to new possibilities that arise endlessly. This is no different from developing your ability to fall and stay in love.

Stepping-Stones to Love
Cleaning the Garbage

1. HOLDING ON

What are you holding on to? What is it that you feel you absolutely need, adore, can't live without? Take a moment and look at this. (It can be something in the outside world, or a person, a memory, a desire or a dream.) Now take another moment and see the effect this is having in your life. What is this keeping away from you? Just take a good look.

2. HOLDING ON IN RELATIONSHIPS

Now take a look at what you are holding on to in your relationships. What do you feel is absolutely necessary in a relationship, that you couldn't live without? Realize this is baggage you carry that not only keeps away all kinds of people and possibilities, but makes you fearful and rigid.

Let something go. At first let it go it for just one day and see how it feels to be without it. (Remember, you can always take it back again.) Then try it for another day. As we do this, many times we realize that that which we thought was protecting us, was really getting in the way. Find out for yourself.

Now let go of something else. Do the same process with this. Do this as often as you care to. You may begin to feel lighter and happier as this goes on. Things may pop up suddenly that you realize you do not need, that you've been carrying from childhood. View this as a time for exploration and rediscovery of your relationships.

As you do this exercise, you will soon notice room being created for something or someone quite new.

3. CLEANING HOUSE

Go to your physical home and take another long, good look around. What in it needs cleaning or straightening? Is there an area of clutter pushed away somewhere? Are there hiding spots in your home where no one can see what's broken or in need of repair? How about clutter? Look at the objects you have collected. How many of them are being used now? What function are they serving? What message are they giving you day in and day out?

Today choose just one thing to clean up. Clean it up thoroughly. (If it is clutter in even one drawer, remove every last shred. If it is a pot that needs cleaning, do what Soen Roshi advises.) It's not advisable to overwhelm ourselves with demands to do everything at once. If you choose just one task a day, you will be amazed at how you will feel at the end of the week, then after two weeks—and three.

Do this cleaning mindfully, slowly, thoroughly. Realize that as you are cleaning your outer space, you are cleaning your inner world as well.

4. A SINGLE SPOT

What is the single spot in your life that is hidden somewhere out of sight and needs some cleaning? Take a moment and recognize it. (Also notice what the single spot is in your relationship, the one no one will mention.) Notice the effect it may be having upon all of your life. Give it a little time in the light. Spend time looking at it. Recognize that it's not so bad, not so hard to clean up. Start cleaning it today, just a little bit. If you do a little day by day, before you know it, this spot will lose its power over you and your relationships.

5. OPEN SPACE

How much open, empty, clean space can you tolerate? How attached are you to the objects in your life, to the clutter? Take a little while to realize this. What are these objects doing for you? A little child loves to cling to his blanket, hat, bottle or mommy for security. What is it that makes you feel secure? This is a very large question that we will address in many forms throughout the rest of the book. It is a crucial question to ask yourself in the matter of relationships. Unless we can feel secure in ourselves, relationships may simply become another security blanket for us. This works against the aliveness and joy of being able to fall and stay in love.

Today, decide to feel secure in your relationship. Realize you are a worthwhile person, whether your partner stays or goes away. Realize that you can have a full, happy life with or without this particular person. In fact, it is essential for you to do so. Do not lean upon your partner for security. Find the true source of your security now.

Chapter 6

BEING THE DOORMAN
(being there for others)

Give up, sirs, your proud airs, your many wishes, mannerisms and extravagant claims. They won't do you any good, sir. That's all I have to tell you.
—LAO-TZU

EVERYONE WANTS TO BE IMPORTANT. We all want to be welcomed, appreciated and desired. In fact, when we receive a great deal of this approval from someone, the high that follows is often mistaken for being in love. Many of us begin to crave that person, crave how we feel in his presence. Often what we are craving, however, is not the other person. We are craving the high his ego is providing, the temporary sense of being wonderful. We are not really in love with the other, but have simply fallen in love with a beautiful image of ourselves and end up judging the success of the relationship by how special we feel.

It's important to take a moment here and see what this *high* really consists of—why many seem to crave it so deeply, and how it's radically different from truly being in love.

HIGH ON THE APPROVAL OF OTHERS

We ascribe more reality to how others see us, than to how we see ourselves. This is viewing ourselves as an object, losing the heart of who we truly are.
—JEAN-PAUL SARTRE

Many of us are addicted to the high we get from the approval of others. Right from the cradle we are taught to perform all kinds of tricks to receive love and attention. The idea that we must keep performing in order to be worthy of love stays with many of us forever. We often behave differently depending on our audience, or say one thing and think another, buy the right clothes, drive a great car and search for a partner we can walk down the street with who will make us look good. The more approval we have from others, the better person we think we are. Very few realize that this is one of the greatest impediments to falling and staying in love.

Part of the high is knowing ourselves through the eyes of another. But this is a double-edged sword. If others look at us with eyes of praise, we feel confident. If they look at us critically or with disappointment, we become disappointed in ourselves. If others do not look at us at all, we may feel we do not exist.

If one's sense of self is obtained through the eyes of another it is always subject to being lost. The person who admires us so much one moment may suddenly lose his taste for us the next day. Or, we may develop new qualities that do not happen to suit him. Any number of circumstances can arise to alter the balance and cause us to lose this wonderful sense of who we are.

This is precisely why relationships often start wonderfully and begin to falter a few months down the road. As partners start revealing different qualities, they look at each other with new eyes. Criticism develops. The thrill of their unwavering adoration begins to dissipate like the air in a fragile balloon. Though painful and often shocking, losing this thrill is not so bad. When we love someone because he adores us, needless to say, this is not love. It isn't healthy and most likely will not last long.

A monkey sitting at the edge of a pond saw the reflection of the moon in the water. Entranced, he reached out for it, digging into the water, splashing around. The more he splashed, the further it eluded him, broken into pieces by the waves he made. The monkey never knew this was only a reflection. Finally, in desperation to touch the moon, he flung himself into the water and drowned. If only the monkey had stopped splashing and looked up for a moment, he could have seen the real moon in the sky.

—ZEN STORY

When we stop splashing around in the water of love, let go of our crazed hunger for approval and stop seeking our own reflection in the eyes of our partner, we begin to discover who we truly are. From there it is only a step or two to being able to easily fall in love.

In Zen practice every person is the right person to love, just as she is. The sense of self that arises through Zen practice is different. It is based upon that which is real and lasting, not upon anything that can ever be lost. In Zen this self is also called the "true man of no rank." It is the self that is not dependent upon approbation or external circumstances to feel whole and joyous. In good and bad weather it goes on its way, unconcerned.

JUST BEING PRESENT: A ZENDO LESSON

The natural is right.
The easy is right.
To be yourself is right.
To be yourself is all that you can
    really be.
Anything else is to go astray.

—BHAGWAN SHREE RAJNEESH

One of the most important jobs at the zendo, though many do not realize it, is being the doorman. This job is rotated, so that on different evenings, different individuals undertake it. The doorman stands at the door of the zendo, quietly and unobtrusively, mostly looking down. When someone arrives she sometimes nods, often does nothing. If the person entering has a question, such as where to put his shoes or his bag, the doorman quickly takes care of it. Other than that, the interaction is minimal.

The doorman does not assert her personality. She make no demands upon the person entering, but simply provides a presence at the door. This presence tells the person who is arriving that he is not alone. He is not entering helter-skelter a place unprepared to greet him. There is someone there welcoming him. It also tells him that, like the doorman, he does not have to perform all kinds of antics to be welcome. He can enter, exactly as he is.

Many people are used to giving and giving, to watching a person's every single mood and need, anticipating his desires. There isn't anything they won't do to keep another happy, to keep the person from going away. Even the sight of someone coming to see them can throw them into frantic activity, trying to please. They do not realize how ill at ease this makes others. They need to stop to question whether others want or need what they are giving. Their hunger for approval fuels their every act.

Margaret was confused by the fact that her tactics didn't work. No matter how much she gave them, ultimately the men in her life left anyway. She had little awareness that her giving was not giving, and she had no idea of the demand she was making upon others by behaving in this way. Unconsciously, she was expecting others to treat her as she treated them, to feel beholden to her so they could not leave. What Margaret saw as being giving was truly spinning a web of control.

In their relationships, these individuals become a doormat (rather than a doorman) because they live focused upon others out of the desperate fear of not being loved. Not knowing who they really are, they have no idea what they have to truly offer. In this process, they do not realize how deeply they are rejecting and turning away from themselves.

THE GREATEST GIFT

By standing there silently, in touch with her own breathing and serving others by simply being there, the doorman can demand nothing. The person entering does not have to please her, pay attention to her or return her overly warm smiles and greeting. The person arriving is permitted to be there, simply as he is. This is the greatest gift the doorman can give a visitor, though it may take a while to realize it.

In relationships, the way we enter is of crucial importance as well. Are we just falling in unwelcomed? Is there anyone home waiting at the door? Has the space inside been prepared? Is the person ready? Is it the right time? Is the person demanding we behave in certain ways, or is there room for us to be who we are?

All those who enter relationships must know what they are getting into. The way a relationship starts often tells you all you need to know about what is going to follow. Don't overlook the beginning. Pay attention to details and tone. Listen to what the person says to you about who he is and what he wants. So many brush aside these beginning communications, believing they will be able to change or mold the person in time.

When we pay attention to the start of our relationships, there is no limit to what is possible. We are not viewing the other as an object to make us happy or fulfill our endless desires. In the same manner we, too, are not there as an object. The other is being allowed to enter in his full personhood, and we are allowed to retain our full personhood as well. Unlike the monkey, splashing in the pond, we are not grabbing at the other to fill us up, or make our lives worthwhile. We are there simply to be together.

By setting up a situation of safety, acceptance and great respect, we clear the space for old patterns to fall away, and a new taste of love to arise.

Margaret, a thirty-four-year-old social worker, always had the same issue in her relationships. She always found herself going out on a limb to be there for her boyfriends, to listen to them when they called with problems and attend events that were important to them. But when it came time for them to be there for her—even for something minor—they inevitably disappointed her, usually coming up with some convenient excuse. Her relationships felt like a one-way street, and she couldn't see them changing. But this is what she felt was needed in order to be loved.

Margaret did not understand the dynamics of truly being there for another, confusing masochistic subservience with true giving. A therapist might say that Margaret simply did not feel worthy of receiving appropriately in a relationship. The element of abusiveness in her pattern suggests that Margaret had significant unconscious guilt, and felt she should be punished and deprived, rather than loved by her partner.

Margaret is not alone. Many who do not feel good about themselves will constantly perform in a relationship, no matter what is or is not being returned. Many people who feel guilty about receiving love, and unworthy of it, find their relationships filled with punishment. This removes the guilt they feel and balances the scales. Self-sacrifice is the price they pay for receiving the love they long for.

Margaret struggled with her guilt and unworthiness, trying hard to overcome it, telling herself she was a good person. Over and over she repeated affirmations such as, "I am a good person, deserving of love." She was building up a new sense of herself, trying to become another person, someone different, someone worthy of love. Margaret had to exert great effort to maintain this new identity, not allowing the truth of who she felt she was to slip back in. She thought that if she finally could see herself as deserving, the right man would enter her life.

At this point Margaret did not see that nothing extra was needed. She was deserving of love just as she was. She didn't have to create a false personality. Love was not about gaining approval in the eyes of others.

When Margaret came to the zendo and was assigned the role of the doorman, she became free from presenting a false image to the outer world, and she simultaneously freed others as well. By virtue of her natural presence, by not intruding or judging others as they entered, she gave them all they needed.

DISSOLVING FEAR OF ABANDONMENT

Different people react to the role of the doorman in different ways. Bob had a great fear of loneliness. When he took on the role of doorman, he felt like a fool. "I thought I was being rotten," he said. "Not looking, smiling or cheering them up, I felt I was ignoring others, leaving them alone to fend for themselves."

Although Bob did all he could to get out of the job, the Zen master insisted that he take it. In fact, he had to do it twice as often as the others.

"I feel like I'm abandoning everyone," he complained.

"So abandon them," the Zen master said.

Many fear both abandoning others and being abandoned. Their entire relationships revolve around this fear. As one does the job of the doorman this issue comes straight to the fore. What does it mean to really be there for another, or to keep another satisfied? Does it mean meeting all their desires and needs, pretending to be someone you're not?

By doing the job of doorman, our illusions about ourselves and others become clear. We do not act upon the feelings, however; we just stay focused upon what is required of us. By staying focused upon the job we are given, the painful feelings arise and then depart. Soon Bob could see he was not abandoning anyone by being with himself. He saw how freeing it was for everyone, and how rewarding it was for him as well. Soon it became easy to see how his fear of being abandoned and abandoning others had driven his life.

When you feel you are abandoning another by being who you are, or that you are not enough for him, realize that this is an illusion. Who you are is always enough. If your partner wants something different, it does not reflect upon you, but upon his needs and fantasies. Twisting yourself into a pretzel to satisfy the fantasy of others simply distorts your own being and never satisfies them in the long run anyway. Although a relationship may not be suitable and two people may not fit together, one person can never ultimately be the cause of another's loneliness.

UNDERSTANDING LONELINESS

In social moments we see how estranged
we are from each other.
—PAUL TILLICH

The only real loneliness comes from abandoning ourselves, from not being who we are. Then we turn to another to fill us. When we operate in this fashion, no matter how many people are in our world, we feel abandoned and alone.

Loneliness or a sense of alienation and misunderstanding are the primary complaints we hear in relationships. Many wives feel lonely with their husbands even when they are together in a room. Individuals in relationships frequently claim that their partners do not know who they truly are. Communications are either one-sided, or not forthcoming at all. People spend hours trying to figure what their partner is really thinking or meaning. Many report that their partner can tolerate just so much intimacy and no more. They are close one moment, then start withdrawing. This merry-go-round continually leaves people wondering when and how to get off.

"There is nothing worse than being in a relationship with someone you care for and feeling alone," said Marsha after having been with Doug for three years. "I love him. I don't want to leave him, but these days I feel more lonely with him than when I am alone." It is common to think that when we are close to another, when they are interacting with us fully, our loneliness will dissolve. From the Zen point of view, this is upside-down thinking. Although our sense of loneliness is temporarily masked at the times we feel close to our partner, it is not really gone, and will arise again when conditions change. The more we flee from it, the more it will remain.

Marsha stays in the relationship because anything feels better to her than being alone. She can't bear the thought that if she leaves, she will never find anyone again. The paradox of this sad situation is that, right now, Marsha is alone despite her relationship. The physical presence of another only masks what is going on. By mistaking loneliness and aloneness, many of us make a vital mistake.

For many the hardest part of being a Zen student is sitting alone on the cushion. Even though the zendo is filled with people, unless they are in personal contact with them, they feel lonely and empty. They constantly fight the urge to turn, look at or talk to those sitting nearby. But they must learn to fully be with their sense of emptiness and loneliness before they can have a true relationship.

Rather than escape from the loneliness by interacting others, Zen students make friends with it as they sit on the cushion and discover what loneliness truly is. They begin to taste the essential loneliness of the human condition: the seasons change, time passes and those we love leave our lives. This is called the pain of transience. However, we can change this loneliness to aloneness. There is a world of difference between them.

MOVING BEYOND LONELINESS INTO ALONENESS

> Sweeping the temple garden
> The voice of autumn
> Getting deeper day by day.
> —SOEN ROSHI

In order to overcome the pain of transience we must learn the difference between loneliness and being alone. Unless we can be alone with ourselves, unless we can recognize and accompany ourselves, be at one with the changes life entails, no matter how many are with us, we will always remain lonely.

This is not to suggest we become a recluse or a hermit, or someone who has rejected companionship. Just the opposite. We must simply learn to become whole and complete within ourselves, free to be with or without a companion, free to depend upon ourselves, know who we are, not be led around by others, but walk freely on our own two feet on this precious earth.

When you are able to do that, you do not have to protect a false image of yourself in order to feel lovable. All of life will then become precious to you because you have accepted and treasured your own real self. When you can become your own companion, then relationships become wonderful adventures, not something you cling to in order to survive. Now you can love all who come before you. You can see who they are, appreciate, rejoice. You can share your fullness with them, and when the time for parting comes, you can let go naturally.

Stepping-Stones to Love
The Simple Self

1. MOST IMPORTANT MOMENTS

Stop a moment and become aware of what the most important moments and aspects of your relationships are to you. Be honest with yourself when you do this. What is it you crave in your relationships? What does this make you feel about yourself? What is it you feel?

This exercise shows us the underpinnings of our relationships, what we use them for. When we can stop using our relationships for personal validation, we begin to build an honest, lasting relationship with our true selves.

2. DEMANDS OF OTHERS

What do you demand of others in order to allow them to enter your life? What kind of person or behavior is unacceptable to you? This is not to suggest that you allow everyone and anyone into your world. It is only to make you aware of what you will and will not accept—what will cause you to leave a relationship. It will also make you aware of what you are unconsciously, or consciously, requiring of your partner and of yourself. See if your list is reasonable.

See if it is all as you would wish it to be. See how your demands will narrow or broaden the possibilities for you—and if you could possibly let some of them go.

3. GIVING GIFTS

What gifts do you give others in relationships? What do you give unnecessarily that may not be wanted or appreciated? Take a few moments to see what motivates your giving. Take a few moments to see what you hope to receive in return.

Now spend time noticing what you have to give that is easy and natural for you, part of who you are. Is this enough? Is it welcomed? Can you choose to have relationships with those who want what you have to offer, with those who appreciate your particular gifts?

4. BEING THERE

In what ways are you willing to be the "doorman" in your relationships? In what ways are you willing not to impose or intrude on another, but just be available for him as he is? Make a list of these. Look the list over. Then each day, see if you can do this for someone else. Let the person just be there, a whole world unto himself. And let yourself be there as well, with your whole world. Don't leave yourself behind when they appear. Don't leave them behind either.

See how you feel when you are behaving this way, and see how the other reacts. At first it may seem odd to you, but keep it going for a while. Great surprises may appear.

5. LONELINESS AND ALONENESS

When are you lonely in your life? What do you do to deal with it? This is very important to realize. Are you willing to experience your loneliness directly? If you are willing not to move and to fully experience it, your loneliness will turn into aloneness. From the basis of aloneness you are strong. All kinds of relationships are then possible.

We are constantly invited to be what we are.
—HENRY DAVID THOREAU

Chapter 7

COOKING
(nourishing others and oneself)

To care for things makes the whole world come to life.
—UCHIYAMA ROSHI

IT'S DELICIOUS TO FEEL well nourished in relationships. There's a yearning and hunger we bring to our partners for all kinds of emotional sustenance: warmth, kindness, appreciation, time spent together. As long as nourishment is forthcoming, our relationships please us and make us feel secure. However, when food is not forthcoming, or the quantity diminishes, some will do anything they can to get fed. Some individuals start hunting for new loves, others beg their partners for food. There are those who become resigned to living on a starvation diet. A few just curl up and starve.

Right from the moment we are born, we connect being fed with being loved. When we cry, Mother comes and feeds

us and we feel safe and cared for. If the food we need is withheld for too long, we believe she doesn't love us, or is withholding food to punish. The world is unwelcoming and our
very survival may be at stake. Some never know what to do
to get the love and nourishment they need.

GETTING FED

This primal paradigm can continue throughout an entire
life. Both men and women frequently perceive their partner
the same way they perceived their mother, and the relationship becomes about getting fed. The role of mother and
child alternates in some relationships. In other cases one
person consistently plays the role of the feeder and the other
the role of the one being fed. Some withhold love so their
partner will do what they want of them. Others feed their
partners on demand in order to keep them happy, then become drained, feeling their partner is insatiable. Sex is often
used in this fashion. It is a primary source of emotional food
for many, providing a sense of being loved, wanted, cared
for and nourished. When it is withheld or rationed out, the
hungry partner feels devastated.

Many individuals do not know if they have a right to
"want more" from their relationships. Are they being
greedy? Is it possible that no matter how much they are
given, they will never feel happy and full? Or are they suffering from emotional indigestion, the inability to fully take in

and absorb that which is offered to them? Such doubts arise in large numbers of relationships. Many have a hard time gauging what exactly they are receiving and why they still feel discontent.

Most are not aware of the many kinds of emotional nourishment the universe abundantly provides. As in childhood, they become fixated on one person, whom they see as their sole source of well-being. They transfer this desperate attitude to their relationships, believing all of their nourishment can be provided by one person only: their particular mate.

In order to understand the true dynamics of relationships, how to fall and stay in love, we must understand the real process of nourishment—of cooking and being fed.

The first thing to notice is our intense orientation toward *receiving.* The feeling is that in order to feel full and nourished, we must be fed. This is the idea of the infant—feed me and all will be well.

Lester, a man in his sixties, joined a dating service, and due to his age, buoyant demeanor and big yellow Cadillac, received one introduction after the next. After each date, he was asked to report back about how the evening went. Lester went on many dates without saying much about them. Finally, the service received a glowing report. "What an evening," reported Lester. "She's everything I ever wanted. I went to her house for a home-cooked dinner, and what did she show me when I got there? A freezer full of steaks." This was a match made in heaven for Lester. He envisioned a lifetime of being fed.

Some relationships are based only upon the opportunity to be fed, but sooner or later our supply of steaks can begin to grow thin. We must be aware of all kinds of food—emotional, mental and spiritual—that are needed in a complete relationship. A lifetime of steaks may be not be enough. As we mature and ripen many other considerations must be included. It is necessary to stop and take a moment to recognize exactly what kind of food we are consuming in the relationship. Is it healthy, and is it food our system can digest?

WANTING ANOTHER DISH

We must to learn how to recognize, taste and digest the food we are receiving. Although fast food may taste good and initially fill us up, it can have bad side effects. The same is true in relationships. Although what we get from our partner is initially hot and spicy, it can cause heartburn later and erode our sense of well-being. We can eat all day, but if we do not taste and digest what we are eating, we will never receive the nourishment we need. Similarly, we can be with a person forever, but if we do not taste who he really is, and take in what he is offering, how can the relationship satisfy?

Clea spent all her time wanting to change Arnold. "There's so much that's wonderful about him," she said, "but what I'm hungering for, I don't get. I need more excitement. I need romance. I'm dying without it." Rather than go to another relationship where she could get the "excitement" she thought she was missing, she stayed with Arnold, feeling dissatisfied and forlorn.

It was as though Arnold were an apple tree who was giving her fabulous apples, while she was all the time longing for pears. Rather than walk down the street to the pear tree and take one, she railed against this fine apple tree, which could not produce a pear, no matter how hard it tried. You will never turn an apple tree into a pear tree. If you cannot enjoy apples, if you are hungering for pears, you must go and find a pear tree.

Yet some of us are simply addicted to being dissatisfied: we cannot take what is given and say thank you. In order to live a life of being in love, we must learn to take what is given and offer thanks in return. Because there is no food (or relationship) that is digested completely, we must also be able to sort out that which is valuable and eliminate the waste. If we spend all our time wanting to change the person, rejecting his essential qualities, not wanting or valuing what he basically gives, this is a surefire recipe for nausea.

Some relationships are a mixture of delight and despair—that which we love and that which we are allergic to. Are we able to absorb what is useful and discard the rest? Some individuals can do this. Many cannot. Some feel they must take everything in, eat it all up, no matter how their body objects. They not only eat the apple, they chew up and swallow the seeds, core and stem. The same goes for relationships. Do we have to absorb all the person offers? Can we take in the beauty and value offered, and bypass that which is not valuable? Such discrimination takes a high level of maturity. It takes a willingness to realize how to enjoy the fruit of the apple and eliminate the seeds.

In order to do this, we need to know what we are receiving from the person, what is useful and valuable to us and what is not. We then must be able to eliminate that which is not healthy for us, and enjoy that which is. This requires the ability to discriminate, to know who we are and what we need and who the other person is, what he is capable of giving. Because some parts of the person do not agree with our system, this does not mean that we cannot enjoy and appreciate the parts that do. It is a mistake to expect all of our needs to be met by one person or in one relationship. Honor and be grateful for that which you receive. Don't become bitter and spend all your time focusing on that which the person is not able to provide.

THE *TENZO* (THE COOK AT THE ZENDO): A ZENDO LESSON

It is one thing to learn how to find the right food, to absorb and enjoy it. But in order to receive all the nourishment we have ever needed, we must learn how to become the cook— how to nourish and feed others.

In the zendo the cook is called the *tenzo*. During retreats the tenzo prepares all the meals. It is the most central job of *sesshin*. Sesshin is a retreat, which can be one day, three days, one week or even three months long. Usually students arise at four or five in the morning and practice until nine or ten at night. The day includes zazen, kinhin, cleaning, eating, *teisho* (talks given by the master), personal meetings with the master and periods of rest. During this time students do not come or go. They gather together to deepen their practice. In a sense, without the tenzo, the sesshin could not go on at all. No one could continue to do zazen without meals. Without this nourishment it would be difficult to persist during the long hours. During sesshin meals have to be ready exactly the moment the bell rings out, at the end of hours of zazen. The bells announce mealtime. After the meal bell rings, the students get up, walk in kinhin and then receive their meals in the zazen posture, in total silence. The meals are a continuation of the sesshin, not a break of any kind. They must be served at exactly the right moment.

The cook stays in the kitchen throughout most of the sesshin and cooks. Sometimes she may have to feed a hundred people or more. The meals must be cooked with great mindfulness and care, with not a drop of food wasted. The very cooking itself becomes a deep training in offering, not only of the food, but of one's entire self. When one's state of being is absorbed by such a task, it is impossible to be hungry or discontent.

EACH INGREDIENT IS PRECIOUS

In addition to preparing the food carefully, during Zen training we must see and be respectful of the nature of each ingredient. Dogen Zenji, a great Zen master, wrote a book entitled *Instructions to the Cook*. This book is considered seminal in Zen practice. His careful instructions to the cook in handling ingredients must also be understood as instructions for handling the ingredients of our lives and relationships. Each person we meet is another ingredient. One may appear to be a delicacy, another a simple green.

In preparing the food for the community it is crucial not to grumble about the quality of the ingredients, but rather to cultivate a temper which sees and respects them for what they are. A dish is not necessarily superior because you have prepared it with choice ingredients, nor is a soup inferior because you have prepared it with ordinary greens. When handling and selecting greens, do so wholeheartedly, with a pure mind, and without trying to evaluate their quality, in the same way in which you would prepare a splendid feast. In our practice we don't make distinctions between delicacies and plain food. There is just one taste, that of the world itself as it is. Remember, delicious and ordinary tastes are the same, not two. Likewise, realize that a simple green has the power to bring all good to you.

—DOGEN ZENJI, *INSTRUCTIONS TO THE COOK*

WHO WILL DO IT IF I DON'T?

A great Zen master, Dogen, traveled from Japan to China to study Zen. When he arrived at the monastery he was to train at, he saw an old monk, sitting in the hot afternoon sun, drying mushrooms. Dogen stopped at the monk's side.

"It is such a hot afternoon," he said. "Why are you sitting like this here in the sun? Why don't you leave this for a younger monk?"

"This is my work," the old monk replied. "Who will do it if I don't?"

Somehow in life and in relationships we all think we are replaceable, that our particular effort or contribution does not matter very much. We can easily pass our work off to someone else. It doesn't matter if we do it or not. In fact, many of us do our best to pass our jobs off, feeling it is better to relax in the shade and let someone else make the effort—usually the person we're in the relationship with. Who we are, what we have to give and the nature of our particular contribution doesn't even cross our minds.

The old monk was different. He fully realized who he was. He knew that his work was a gift given to him. He knew no one could do it as he did, and beyond that, he understood deeply that caring for life, caring for the mushrooms and hungry people in the zendo, would make his own life worthwhile. His effort and work were not experienced as burdens, they were not something he did to seek glory and fame. It was his privilege to dry the mushrooms.

How many feel this way in their relationships? How many are grateful to give what they have to offer, will work hard under all circumstances to make sure the relationship receives the food it needs? Rather than focus upon what is lacking in the relationship, focus upon what the relationship needs and ways in which you can provide it. When we give to another the care that we want, we open the door to receive it as well.

If communication seems to be lacking, make every effort to communicate. Find the best times and ways to do this. Become aware of what your partner needs in order to be able to hear you. Find new ways of hearing what your partner is trying to say and of responding to him.

In order to become more considerate of your partner, take real account of his needs and wants. As you become more sensitive to and considerate of the other, this will impact you as well. This does not mean having a one-way relationship. It means that when we take responsibility for doing what is needed to build a fine relationship, we are doing the work given to us at this particular time. We are understanding the saying of the old monk, "Who will do it if I don't?"

Samantha, who is thirty, had been dating Rick for two years. She was satisfied with the relationship, although not in love. Something was missing. She couldn't complain that Rick wasn't there for her—he was—it was just that he never seemed to be more than just there. He responded to her needs, but he didn't anticipate them. He listened when she discussed her hopes for a career as an artist, but never actively encouraged her. This was the usual pattern for Samantha's relationships: content, but not in love. Now that she'd turned thirty, she wondered if she should just accept things as they were. Perhaps she had been wrong to ever expect anything more.

In this relationship, Samantha had been living with enough food to sustain her, but not to fill her up. There is a difference between the experience of a mutual flow of understanding and aliveness and a response to whatever a partner needs or wants. Receiving the true attention of another is always the best kind of food. Someone who responds automatically is not truly present in the relationship, but acting passively, out of conditioning or a sense of duty. His partner often feels a flatness and emptiness, a sense that the person is not really there.

Samantha yearned for the experience of being really responded to, not merely placated, but she did not know how to elicit that reaction. She thought maybe she was crazy for even feeling discontent.

"I had no idea," said Samantha, "what it really meant to give before—to truly care about another person."

This insight shocked her. She realized that her entire life orientation had been toward what she could get for herself. Awareness and compassion for the needs of another never truly entered her mind.

When Samantha became a Zen student, she was assigned the job of washing the vegetables during sesshin. Both she and the tenzo were entirely concentrated upon doing their tasks thoroughly and getting them finished by exactly the right moment. As they wordlessly washed and chopped the food, mixed the ingredients and put them on the stove, they kept the kitchen immaculately clean. There was no room for clutter, no time for thinking or complaining about what a huge, impossible job it was, that it wouldn't get done on time. That wasn't even a possibility. Downstairs hungry people were waiting.

"When you're cooking up there with total concentration, you can actually feel the effort of others sitting downstairs. You can also feel their hunger and appreciation when the food is served at the right moment," Samantha said.

As Samantha scraped and chopped the vegetables, she realized at that moment it was her privilege to be doing that. As she stood there and worked, she became grateful for everyone who was sitting there hungry, waiting for the food. She realized how much she was needed, what a difference her work made. Tears ran down her cheeks. She'd never felt this way before.

FEEDING OTHERS, WE ARE FED

Being the cook means learning how to appreciate the needs of others, and being willing to completely fill them, on time. Rather than compulsively focusing on our own hunger, we become naturally aware of the needs of others. As we do this, a strange thing happens: our own hunger completely fades away. Feeding others, we are fed ourselves. We are able to taste life (and people) as they are given. Our relationships turn around 180 degrees. It no longer becomes a question of what the other is or isn't giving. It becomes a question of what can be offered to him or to her. This is tremendously different from the way we usually approach our hunger—our usual desire simply to be fed. As we place our attention upon the needs of others and find ways of giving to them, not only does our hunger subside, but we begin to feel full. We take joy in our ability to bring satisfaction to those we care about. As this process continues, there is a deeper lesson to learn: that a never-ending source of all kinds of nourishment exists within us. We need never feel empty or hungry again.

However, many in relationships have yet to learn this lesson. They wage a subtle battle, a power struggle over who gets what, who gets more, who's in charge, who gets their way. The underlying question is, whose needs are more important? How much is each one giving the other? These people keep careful records about what is going out and coming in. They want the other to be indebted to them, or they give only as much as they feel is the other's due. A relationship based upon indebtedness is one based upon market value. Love becomes a commodity to be bought or sold. This never leads to a life of falling in love.

In order to change your orientation, stop counting what

you are giving or receiving; stop worrying about being on top. There is no need to keep thinking about what your partner owes you, just take whatever is given and say thank you. Don't look for one drop more. In addition, don't judge to see whether your partner is worthy of receiving the gifts you have to give. This kind of tactic makes you bitter, resentful, withholding and tied up in a knot. This is not the way to live a life of being in love.

As a great Zen poet said, "Open your hands if you want to be held." Give fully without reservation, without watching what you get back. The more you give, the fuller, happier and more self-sufficient you will become. Much will be returned to you, though not in ways you necessarily expect. Allow the universe to give back to you fully, but do not demand it from any particular person.

THE SECRETS OF TRUE COOKING

The experience of true giving, of really nourishing and being nourished, is often misunderstood. Some individuals often complain that when they give they end up feeling completely drained. "I give and give continuously," they may proclaim, "but receive nothing in return. I'm utterly depleted. I have nothing left to give." This is the position of many martyrs, who act as though in giving, they have lost their entire supply of food or love or joy. They then try to get more by generating guilt. But no one is ever drained by true cooking. And no one ever wants to give to someone out of guilt.

Our misunderstanding of the true nature of nourishing others is what causes our dismay. For most giving is a form of barter: you give to me and I'll give something back to you. We are giving with an ulterior motive, in order to get a return, please others, do what's right. This kind of counterfeit giving is often accompanied by bitterness and the feeling of being "drained." Individuals who feel drained must realize that if they think they are not receiving in return, then they are not truly giving either to others or to themselves.

Whenever giving is a one-sided interaction, a healthy flow of life force is blocked. Some try to hold on by giving to others. Others give gifts that are too costly for them. Some find they have trouble receiving; they only want to give. This, too, is not true giving. There is no greater gift than to receive the gifts and love of another. When we refuse to receive what is offered, we are in effect refusing love. The breath always goes both in and out. We take from the universe and then return what has been received. To breathe in without breathing out, or to breathe out without breathing in, would cause our death.

In a relationship if you are giving and getting nothing back in return, stop *giving* so much, and spend time *being*. Give to yourself, be who you are. Replenish the inner sense—do your own work. Then look to see what you are "using" this relationship for. What are you trying to obtain by giving? Stop trying to obtain anything, and just give with open hands.

In the kitchen, like breathing, true giving and receiving are one. Our very being is validated by a gift that is received and welcomed. When we give fully without wanting anything back in return, we receive as much as we give. Burden, resentment and clinging fall away. There is no giver or receiver here, only an open heart.

As we learn to engage in this kind of giving and receiving, we begin to taste the real fruit of love. Real love makes no claims or demands. It gives what is needed naturally. It cannot be taken away, as it does not belong to anyone. It is as available and plentiful as the air we breathe. In order to taste it, we have only to breathe in and breathe out naturally, in all areas of our lives. It is only the act of refusing to breathe out, to give back to the universe what it has given to us, that keeps all true nourishment away.

PARENTAL MIND

As Zen practice ripens, a student gives easily and naturally. She gives quietly, without seeking recognition and praise. As she becomes more deeply in touch with her true self, she cannot help but nourish others and receive real nourishment as well. This is also called developing "parental mind."

Parental mind is the state of mind that wants to care for and nourish others. It is the mind of the mother with a new-born child, a state of unconditional regard for the world we live in. It is not a mind that keeps accounts or continually needs to be filled up and attended to.

Parental mind develops naturally as we sit in zazen. There is nothing special we need to do to create it. Just by sitting, it is uncovered. By sitting we feed our own deep hunger and become in touch with the flow of nourishment always available to us all. That flow of nourishment can also be called the action of being in love.

Stepping-Stones to Love
Nourishing Self and Others

1. FAVORITE FOOD
What is your favorite food in relationships? What is it you hunger for daily? How do you get fed? Does someone else feed you? Do you feed yourself? Is there some other way you could get this particular nourishment? Take a little while and find out.

2. EMOTIONAL INDIGESTION
What kind of food are you now absorbing in your relationships that you cannot digest? Why do you keep eating it? What do you want from it? Is there some other food that could substitute?

3. COOKING FOR OTHERS

Whom do you cook for usually? Whom is it you are happy to nurture? What kind of food are you providing for him? Do you do it with resentment or with a willing heart? Who else would enjoy being nurtured by you? What stops you from cooking for her as well? Take a little while and consider. What does it do to you to refuse nourishment to someone? Is someone else cooking for her? Who else will do it if you don't?

4. OFFERINGS

What offerings do you bring to life? What are you willing to give unconditionally? Are you receiving joy for doing this? If not, it is not your true offering. Spend time considering what you can truly offer that will nourish and gladden others and you as well. When a large part of our lives consists of making these kinds of offerings, we fall in love with life itself.

5. GIVING GIFTS

Every day, find something new that you can give to somebody. Each day give something else. It does not have to be fancy or expensive, just something that will add to her day. Do this with all kinds of different people. You may also do it with someone you're in a relationship with. Do it quietly and simply, without great fanfare.

Now do it with yourself. Each day take a moment or two to find out what kind of gift you would like today. Then take a little time to give it to yourself. (Once again, these gifts do not have to be fancy or expensive—perhaps a walk in the park, a new book, time to look at watercolors, a long bubble bath.)

Although this exercise is simple, it is extremely powerful. Doing this daily in your relationship can turn everything around. When you give, remember not to look for anything in return (not even a smile or thank-you). Just give to give, no expectations, no demands. This kind of giving is the greatest gift you can experience, and by living with this kind of giving, all kinds of other gifts will come to you in return.

> Dried salmon received
> And oranges given in return.
> —SHIKI

Chapter 8

RECEIVING THE STICK
(dealing with blows)

Do not avoid bitterness.
—SOEN ROSHI

MOST PEOPLE GIVE UP ON RELATIONSHIPS due to fear of pain. After having been shocked, hurt or betrayed one last time, they decide not to try again. Rather than a source of joy and inspiration, relationships become a minefield, where one wrong step causes things to suddenly blow apart. Love becomes associated with shocks and explosions, rejection and loss. In order to be open to falling in love, we must dissolve such fears and see difficulties and disappointments for what they are. Running away isn't the answer. As we run from conflict, we are simultaneously running from all that is worthwhile in our lives. The way we handle the disappointments and the sudden shocks and blows we receive can determine the entire course of both our relationships and our lives.

WHERE DID THE LOVE GO?

The question *Where did the love go?* is the one most commonly asked when people confront changes in a relationship. This question causes great pain as individuals remember the joy they once had and see now how it turned into misery. They have no idea what happened, whose fault it was, where the love went.

The love, of course, didn't go anywhere. Where could it go? Like thunderclouds that roll in, suddenly obstructing the warmth of the sun, waves of negativity and difficulty arise, temporarily cutting off the fundamental love we feel. These waves are not permanent, but part of the ever-shifting panorama of life. From the Zen point of view we must question, who is the host and who is the guest? What, like a guest, comes and goes—is transient—and what, like the host, remains—is absolute?

Without our understanding this point, relationships can never develop from a stable basis. Most people view the temporary manifestation of pain, anger, loneliness and sorrow as the host—the fundamental truth of relationships. In that case, the fundamental presence of love is seen as a temporary manifestation, something that disappears easily. The very opposite is true.

We cannot live a life of love unless we know how to accept the changes that inevitably happen, absorb the blows that are received and place it all in the proper context. As we do this we discover that love never goes anywhere. It is present throughout all permutations. Love is not static, but part of an enormous process that includes pain, joy, bitterness and sweetness. Therefore it is crucial that we become able to receive the changes life presents us in a way that allows us to grow.

> When we parted it broke my heart
> Her powdered cheeks were more beautiful
> than spring flowers.
> My lovely miss is now with another,
> Singing the same love song
> but to a different tune.
>
> —IKKYU

RECEIVING THE STICK: A ZENDO LESSON

At certain points during zazen, a student who has been chosen to be a monitor walks up and down the aisle carrying a big wooden stick called the *keysaku* over his shoulder. As the monitor walks, the students, sitting and doing zazen, have the option of putting their palms together and bowing. This indicates that they are requesting the stick. The monitor then stops, bows to the student and hits him hard on both shoulders, the snapping sound echoing through the zendo. In some zendos, the monitor hits the students whether they request it or not, especially if they seem to be slouching or sleeping on the cushion.

The stick serves many functions. On one level, it releases tension and pain that may have accumulated in the student's shoulders during long hours of zazen. On another level, it sharpens the entire atmosphere of the zendo so that it becomes electric and alert and helps to revitalize it after long, quiet hours of sitting. Most important, it teaches the students how to receive sudden blows and pain. This is necessary, as a fundamental part of learning the art of falling in love is knowing how to receive the stick.

There are many different kinds of blows individuals receive in their relationships: anger, criticism, betrayal, jealousy, loss, sudden change of circumstances. No matter how much love has been expressed between two people, sooner or later something disturbing arises to alter the equilibrium. They may begin to wonder what has really been going on, is the relationship worthwhile, is this really love? Some people have more tolerance than others for blows of these kinds. Many end up wondering, Where did the love go?

PAIN AND LOVE

We eliminate both the doctor and the medicine
by completely accepting the disease.

For some, suffering is inextricably associated with love. The work of therapy is to dislodge the connection between love and pain, to help these people make "healthier" choices, find a partner who will not create so much sorrow in their lives. Sufferers are thought of as patients in the grip of an illness. The process of dislodging them from suffering in relationships is considered the cure.

In Zen practice, the sorrow, shocks and imbalances of life are not seen as an illness. They are not bad, things to be avoided, but rather are to be understood and welcomed as one would welcome a temporary guest. They are not dwelled upon or figured out. They are simply known to be the unavoidable fluctuations of life, like day and night, sun and clouds.

When we label an individual (or situation) as bad, cruel, sick or masochistic, we put the person in a prison without bars. In Zen practice we do not label anyone or anything. The labeling only compounds the problem and prevents the natural flow of change and healing, which is constantly available. By saying a person or situation is fundamentally dark, we obstruct the sun from shining upon her, prevent the thunderclouds of her life from naturally blowing away.

Harriet, who is thirty-six, had finally met someone she was happy with. After three years together, marriage seemed in their future and both were thrilled. Then the blows came. Fred, her boyfriend, had a stroke. It took him many months to recover, and when he finally did, he wasn't the same. He was more withdrawn, a little slower. On top of this, her parents disapproved of the fact that he was Catholic, and never ceased to let this be known. They threatened to boycott her wedding and disinherit her if she married him. Despite all of this, Harriet loved him, felt he would improve further, and wanted somehow to make it work. She just didn't know how many more difficulties she could withstand.

Psychologically speaking, one could say that Harriet had to understand the reasons she was choosing a marriage that would be fraught with problems from the start. Was she staying with her boyfriend out of love, guilt or rebellion against her parents? Was she truly able to sustain the ongoing issues such a union might bring? Harriet had difficulty coming to grips with this because she held on to the belief that a suitable relationship was one where no real hardship existed.

Although Harriet's situation may seem extreme, it is similar to what many people experience in relationships—unexpected shocks and changes, either in the person or in the circumstances. Such trauma can make us feel like a victim of life, but in truth we are only experiencing the loss of the way things once were.

As Harriet came to the zendo and began to learn a new way of being with her life, the intense need to make a decision about her relationship faded into the background. Instead she became occupied with basics, discovering who she truly was, recognizing what was fundamental in her life and what came and went—who was the host and who was the guest.

At the right moment the appropriate action became completely clear. It arose naturally. Every cell in her body told her what to do about her boyfriend, where she wanted to be, what was right for her and what was not. She no longer obsessed or went back and forth about a decision. Clear-cut guidance arose on its own. Harriet decided to remain with her fiancé, whether he improved more fully or not. She realized that she loved him, and the changes he had suffered did not alter that.

IDENTIFYING RELATIONSHIP POISONS

The Buddha said that all suffering (all thunderclouds and afflictions) is caused by the three poisons—greed, anger and delusion—that exist within all of us. These poisons are inherent in the human condition and must be purified. They surface in our lives when appropriate circumstances arise. This is part of our karma—our mental, emotional and physical composition—constructed by ourselves through our deeds, thoughts and actions.

Some of these poisons in relationships express themselves as jealousy, fear, anger, suspiciousness, attachment and possessiveness. We develop fantasies about others that have no basis in reality. These feelings are painful, but they surface in order to be released, not to be acted upon. When we don't understand their true nature, we think these painful feelings are caused by the situation or the other person. We may also feel that these feelings are expressions of our love, that we have a right to feel possessive and attached to the person; anyone in love would feel that way.

We might also think these poisons are part of our identity, who we essentially are. But rather than try to justify these painful moments, we must simply recognize them for what they are and let them go. The great art of relationships is learning how to handle the poisons when they appear. They are the essence of the stick we receive, the blows that hurt us in our relationships.

Our monkey mind may make its objections to handling pain in this way. Our monkey mind loves to dwell upon and intensify difficulties of all kinds. It reacts to everything impulsively and thrives on endless chatter and mental machinations. Our monkey mind is not willing to let pain and difficulties subside easily and give up its fuel. The monkey mind actually enjoys and seeks these poisons as if they were honey itself.

The way in which we receive our sorrows, the way in which we understand what is happening and respond to it, makes the entire difference between heaven and hell. What could turn into a long, convoluted time of anguish or depression can also be experienced differently—simply like a sudden storm crossing our path. A storm is not a personal reflection of who we are. It arises and departs, clearing the air, making room for the sun. When we view the blows we receive in this way, the pain we feel is not compounded and intensified, but instead becomes an accompaniment to an otherwise purposeful day, and purposeful, happy relationship.

This is not to indicate that there are not times when it is appropriate to end a difficult relationship. There are. But even though we may end a relationship, it is not because we are afraid of facing and receiving the difficulties, or looking for a one-sided experience. Our decision arises after all has been experienced from another basis, a deeper part of ourselves.

HOW MUCH SUFFERING IS ENOUGH?

Sometimes knowing how to receive blows is confused with accepting a sadomasochistic relationship. It is crucial to make a distinction here. When we find ourselves in inequitable power struggles, or yield our own strength, autonomy and life force to another, our fear and anger are an avoidance of love. We declare ourselves weak and incapable, or from the other perspective, imagine we have the right to dominate another. Both of these delusions arise from not knowing who we are or how to truly confront the blows that life brings.

In sadomasochistic relationships one partner is dominated and abused and the other does the dominating. (These roles can reverse from time to time.) The one who accepts the harm does so because she has been fixated upon herself as a victim, inadequate and unworthy of love. The guilt she feels then draws the punishment, which temporarily relieves the guilt. This pattern proves once again how unworthy she and her partner are. Clearly, there is nothing loving in this behavior, either to herself or the other.

The one who, out of weakness and fear of his own vulnerability, plays the dominating role often feels vulnerable and out of control. He then responds by feeling that in the name of love he has the right to control and subjugate. Inflicting pain upon others becomes a protection from the pain he is feeling. Not only is this a degradation of the relationship, it is the very opposite of a loving heart.

All these permutations of pain and power struggles in relationships are the result of not knowing how to deal with the blows life offers. Staying in damaging or painful relationships comes about from our unwillingness to really feel, acknowledge and finally let go of pain. Zen teaches us never to yield autonomy or authority for our lives to another person. Each of us contains the wisdom, strength and beauty to handle everything.

You can decide anytime you want to that enough pain is enough. When you feel your pain thoroughly, it is easier to give it up and choose well-being. The choice is always yours. When we create or stay in relationships that are fundamentally damaging and negate the basic principles of love, suffering will follow as day follows night. When we choose to live with the principles of love, though pain may arise briefly, it will not turn into suffering and we will easily attract support and harmony.

CHOOSING TO LET GO

A soldier named Nobushige came to Hakuin (great Zen master) and asked: "Is there really a paradise and a hell?"

"Who are you?" inquired Hakuin.

"I am a samurai," the warrior replied.

"You, a soldier!" exclaimed Hakuin. "What kind of ruler would have you as his guard? Your face looks like that of a beggar."

Nobushige became so angry that he began to draw his sword, but Hakuin continued: "So you have a sword! Your weapon is probably much too dull to cut off my head."

As Nobushige drew his sword Hakuin remarked: "Here open the gates of hell!"

At these words the samurai, perceiving the master's discipline, sheathed his sword and bowed.

"Here open the gates of paradise," said Hakuin.

—FROM *ZEN FLESH, ZEN BONES,*
COMPILED BY PAUL REPS AND NYOGEN SENZAKI

Anger, fear, jealousy, betrayal, suspiciousness, possessiveness and loss are all part of the human spectrum. Though we experience them vividly in relationships, these unwanted companions accompany us wherever we go. They are part of our ongoing reactions to life. It is up to us to let them go.

Some individuals exacerbate the pain they are feeling by

reacting like Nobushige, producing more anger and negativity. These individuals focus only upon the negative. They take every blow they receive and expand it, covering the relationship with a cloud of darkness. In this way the wound keeps bleeding and their sense of powerlessness intensifies. These individuals have not yet chosen to let go.

Others search for the culprit, vow to get revenge, blame others or blame themselves. Casting blame happens so often that it merits closer examination. Blame directed at the self grows into gnawing guilt and feelings of inadequacy that persist for years on end. The deep sense of failing gets in the way of loving again. Blaming others tarnishes our ability to see the full picture of the other person or ourselves and what truly went on between us. It also keeps bitterness alive so that the moment something unpleasant happens, we are always ready to pull out our sword.

Another way of dealing with these painful feelings is simply to hide, fantasize, withdraw or pretend nothing is happening. These people cover the pain they are feeling with false, shallow smiles. Their partners feel it is impossible to ever get anything resolved with these individuals who refuse to admit anything is wrong. Such denial makes it impossible for a relationship to ever be real. The coat of sugar prevents both partners from sharing who they really are and what is true for them. This kind of relationship is always dissatisfying because it functions on the most superficial level of life.

None of these ways of relating are useful. Instead it is necessary to choose to fully feel what is happening in the moment and then to let go. See it as a storm that is passing, do not cling to the painful emotion and do not let it cling to you. Anger can be seductive. Choose not to be seduced. Refuse to blame another and refuse to blame yourself. When anger arises, refuse to take action at that moment (or to speak words of hate). Realize you are in the center of a storm. Stay in the center quietly while the storm whirls around. When the storm has passed, new understanding will appear and both you and your partner will remain unharmed.

Fantasies and pretense are also seductive, but yield nothing of value. When fantasies arise, or the desire to pretend that all is well, refuse this kind of deception. Stand still and allow yourself to be with the reality of the situation until the desire to escape has vanished. You will grow stronger and clearer about what action to take.

By not reacting to these blows and seductions we are receiving, we remove their fuel and dispel them from our lives.

PULLING OUT THE POISON ARROWS

When the Buddha was asked who he was, he said he was a doctor coming to cure the ills of the world. He said we have all been shot with poison arrows (afflictions, delusions) and he had come to show us how to pull the arrows out. He did not say he would pull them out for us. Part of the agony of our lives and relationships is waiting for someone to pull out our poison arrows, make us feel good and take away our pain. In fact, this is the basis of many relationships. Some even refuse to go on in life until someone comes along whom they can lean upon. This leaning, depending mind only causes the suffering to go deeper. It only causes our relationships to fall apart sooner or later.

In Zen practice we do not depend on others, but learn instead how to connect with our intrinsic strength and wisdom and pull out our own poison arrows. We learn to stand upon our own two feet, chew our own food, sing our own songs and walk bravely upon the earth. This must be the basis of our relationships as well. A relationship based upon two people leaning on one another, begging the other to take away the pain, or demanding that one be weak and the other strong, can only end in disaster. A true love relationship always gives us strength and never takes our autonomy away.

INCLUDING THE BITTER
AND THE SWEET

> A feeling that is strong one moment
> and gone the next
> Cannot be said to be love.
>
> —KABIR

The human condition is to be constantly subject to both the bitter and the sweet. However, when the sweet comes along we want to hold on to it and ensure it will remain with us forever. When bitter times come we want to push them away, numb ourselves, withdraw. From the Zen point of view a bitter taste is bitter, a sweet taste is sweet. In the course of life, we must taste everything. If we spit something out, more will just come later on.

To seek only the good and to reject that which is painful is the way most of us live our lives. This way of living keeps us forever lopsided, cutting much of our experience away. It keeps us in a false cocoon of safety, which is always broken into anyway. Not only relationships, but also life itself is filled with sudden shocks and blows. Our most cherished expectations go awry. This is the nature of cherished expectations. The most unexpected wonders are a step away. That is the nature of unexpected wonders. By refusing to taste bitterness as well as honey, we are refusing to be part of the ineffable nature of love itself.

We learn how to taste everything in the zendo. We enjoy the beautiful sound of the gong when it rings, and we receive the sting of the stick when the time comes for that. We do not add anything to what we are experiencing. The gong does not ring out because we deserve it, the stick does not sting because we are bad. A bitter taste is simply bitter. A feeling of pain is just a feeling of pain. It is not the world crashing down around us. We do not torment ourselves with confusion and guilt. If we feel pain at some juncture, it does not mean we are worthless or that love has forever gone. In fact, it may be said that love is not a feeling at all—it is the ability to be at home with all that comes to us.

In the zendo, when we sit we learn to honor and make friends with all of ourselves and all of life, including our suffering. It is not "love" or "relationships" that cause our sorrows, but the inability to embrace it all. A famous Zen saying goes:

> To separate what we like from what we dislike
> is the disease of mind.
> —SOSAN GANCHI ZENJI

The disease of the mind is to constantly reject one part of ourselves, of others or of our experiences. We say this experience is good and that one is bad. I hate this and love that. I will seek this and turn away from that. This very way of life itself is the illness. It causes us to split from both ourselves and our lives.

As we practice we learn how to thoroughly experience what is happening moment by moment, and soon realize that if we are completely with each moment, the next breath will bring something new. When we do not reject our suffering, or add anything to it, pain is simply pain. It is what we add to it that turns it into suffering, makes it thick and solid, so that it can't subside.

COMPLETION

What we are describing is the experience of completion. This means feeling in a relationship as if one has done and experienced all there was for her to do. One has allowed the other person to truly know her, and she has known him as well. The relationship has been fulfilled. If the relationship is ended, she may miss the person, but she will not mourn so deeply. She will not leave the relationship full of scars. The person and the love they shared will have become a part of her now; something vital will have been integrated.

At first it may seem overwhelming or impossible to complete a relationship. One may feel a sense of futility that no matter what she says or does, the person won't respond, or it won't really change anything. But this is not so. Even just one moment of being present and truthful begins to dissolve so much pain and confusion.

It does not matter if the other person does or does not respond as you wish. One's own act of truthfulness releases one from a sense of pain and futility, regardless of her partner's response. And, in some subtle way, the other will feel it as well.

OPENING THE GATES OF HEAVEN

As awareness increases, as our ability to be present and complete ripens, our Buddha nature (divine nature) manifests. Our potential for health, clarity and love matures and the gates of heaven open. We become able to discern who the person truly is in our relationship and whether we're staying in it for the right reasons or for reasons that are not suitable any longer. We do not leave because we are rejecting another (or in response to rejection), but because the natural flow of our lives is moving us elsewhere. We do not carry traces of bitterness and anguish along with us either, or project them upon the next person. We are able to be aware of the beauty, joy and wonder of all life. We can laugh when we're happy and cry when we're sad. We become one with the sound of the birds, the touch of a friend, the heat of summer, the loss of a dream, the new buds of spring—whatever comes.

This open experience of life can bring us all the healing, joy and strength we need for everything.

Stepping-Stones to Love
Dealing with Pain

1. WHERE DO THE BLOWS COME FROM?

Many times we are suddenly upset or discouraged and don't realize why. It feels as though something has come up from behind us and taken our joy away. Now, take a moment and notice where the blows come from in your life. What do you experience as difficult to bear? Notice your usual reaction to this. Right now, just noticing is plenty. Each day, spend a little time doing this.

2. RELINQUISHING BLAME

Whom or what do you blame for the difficulties you are facing? In what ways do you blame yourself? Make a list. Notice how blaming simply serves as a screen, preventing you from seeing the full picture of what is going on. See how you think it may even be protecting you.

Relinquish some blame today. Go to the top of your list, and completely let go of blaming that person or circumstance. Breathe deeply as you do this. Send the person good wishes. View the situation much as you would view a thunderstorm in your life that came and went. Do you blame the rain for falling?

3. REFUSING TO REFUSE

What do you refuse to experience in life? If you experienced it, what do you think would happen? Imagine experiencing it. Now, imagine it again. Notice how much energy you expend by keeping this experience away. Notice how much bigger you make it than it really is. Then, one day when you are ready, see if you can allow a taste of this experience into your life. What does it feel like? How about you? How much larger and stronger do you feel now?

4. HEALING A WOUNDED RELATIONSHIP

Is there a relationship you are in (or have been in) that is in need of healing? Have blows been given and received that have not yet been released or forgiven? This is a wonderful time to heal it. Take time to review this relationship and see what went wrong in it. Do you need to ask forgiveness of someone? Do you need to offer forgiveness? (To yourself or to another?) Decide today that you will do it. Call or write to the person. (If the person is not alive, you can still do this either in your mind or by writing him or her a letter. Or, if you feel you owe the person a debt, repay that debt now to someone who is living.)

Ask yourself what is needed in order for this relationship to feel healed and complete for you. Don't rush in your answers. Are there gifts that need to be given? Are there gifts you wish you had received? If there are gifts to be given, give them. If there are gifts to be received, see if you can request them. If you can't, or if they won't be forthcoming from that person, see if you can give them to yourself, receive them from another or become aware of other gifts that person has given to you. Sometimes we have received a great deal more in a relationship than we are aware of. Take time to review what you received from this person and what you gave to him or her.

All of this is part of the process of forgiveness. Without forgiveness our lives become clogged, our health impaired and our ability to love restricted. The power, energy and freedom obtained by healing wounded relationships is enormous. As soon as this is done fully, many new doors open.

Some enjoy this process so much they do it daily, much as they would take a bath or shower, refreshing all of themselves. Once you become used to it, you can't do without it. It is the sure road to leading a life of love.

5. SAYING YES

What do you totally say yes to in your life? What can you be with 100 percent? If there isn't anything, then pick something you would like to be able to do this with. Now do it. Put yourself in the presence of whatever it is (person, animal, plant, situation) and in your mind say yes to it! Open up your arms and heart. Open up your mind. Let go of all reservations. Feel yourself expanding like the branches of a huge tree. Say, yes, yes, yes again.

Tomorrow find something else you can do this with. When you do this practice regularly, something wonderful happens. Before long, you'll love the way it makes you feel. You'll start doing it in unexpected places, with people you may have even just met. Or when you get really seasoned at it, you may even do it with someone who's giving you a hard time. Now you are on the road to something special. This way of being doesn't have to be confined. You are getting ready to say yes to all of life. (Is there a better prayer than this, or a better way to bless someone?)

> Sometimes we receive the power to say yes to life and ourselves. The peace enters us and makes us whole.
> —RALPH WALDO EMERSON

Part Three

ADVANCED TRAINING

Chapter 9

SESSHIN: INTENSIVE TRAINING PERIOD
(developing endurance)

We cannot know if it is gold
Until we see it through the fire.
—ZEN SAYING

WITHOUT A DOUBT, life itself is a sesshin, an intense training period, beginning the moment we are born and continuing until we take our last breath. It goes on and on, one day following the next. No matter how we feel—how tired, confused, irritated or upset—we do not get time out. Most are aware that their time will last only so long. Yet, in the midst of life and relationships, time can seem endless, repetitive and even pointless. Some lose sight of why they're here, what they're doing and or how they got so entwined with the particular person or relationship they are in.

Some become desperate for a way out. Others believe a reprieve is possible, that they can drop out for a few years and come back when a situation has resolved itself. There are those who leave a relationship behind when the going gets too rough. Others act out, trying to make the relationship the way they want it by changing all the rules. Others refuse to join the activities. Years pass, opportunities slip by and the sweet taste of love eludes them.

Beyond all else, one thing is needed to get through both sesshin and life successfully, and that is the ability to endure—to have persistence and determination. In order to do that, at some point we must see the larger picture, why we are here at all, what the purpose of sesshin is and what is the purpose of our life.

The same is true in relationships. Without having a grasp of the larger picture, of our purpose in the relationship, it can be a challenge to endure the difficult periods. We begin to wonder what we're doing there and look for ways to get free or find other distractions. However, in order to maintain love in relationships, we must be able to deal with the ongoingness of daily life, with routine and boredom. We must ultimately understand where our real joy and aliveness come from.

CONTINUALLY SEEKING NEW RELATIONSHIPS

Many who continually find fault with the relationships they are in and seek new ones do so for reasons other than those they imagine. They do it not necessarily because their partner is a poor match, but because they are craving entertainment, an escape from the basic reality of daily life. These individuals seek new relationships because they are afraid of staying right where they are, going deeper, becoming vulnerable and experiencing true connection and intimacy. Yet without the ability to do this, it is impossible to really fall and stay in love.

Leaving one relationship for another is often justifiable. We can find endless reasons to find a new partner—someone richer, better, smarter, sweeter—but our reasons seldom make much difference in the long run. The same need to change partners will emerge later on, until we have come to understand the very essence of love itself. Love can feel wonderful in the beginning when it is full of excitement and romance, but when two people have settled into their usual, daily routines, without constant change and distraction, that is the time they must understand the magic of plain life.

SESSHIN: A ZENDO LESSON

As the Zen student's practice develops, it becomes natural for her to attend *sesshin*. Sesshin is a period of intense training. Sitting usually begin at four or five in the morning and last until nine at night, with breaks for meals, work and resting. There is no talking, interacting or coming and going. You are not allowed to leave. Sesshins can last for one day, one weekend, one week or three months. A one-hundred-day period is known as *kesai*. Zen monks attend kesais regularly.

During sesshin we focus upon nothing but practice. All outside demands, distractions and entertainment are removed. This is a time to harness our scattered energies and go deeper in dealing with the reality of our lives and ourselves. It is a time to develop patience and endurance, and to become senior to all the pain, conflicts and other phenomena that accost us continually—boredom, sameness of routine, lack of distraction, change. From morning until night, during sesshin we do the same things again and again. Of course, one can also view a relationship as a sesshin, and apply the same principles.

Our life is reduced to fundamentals. During sesshin there is no opportunity to get lost in the whirl. We get up, wash, sit, breathe, walk, drink, eat and go to the bathroom. We do the simple cleaning jobs assigned to us in order to keep our environment immaculate. We rest at the appointed time, then we get up and do the whole thing once again. These basic life activities, which most of us either try to avoid or rush through, become the door to learning what it means to love.

In a sense we are going back to kindergarten, learning

how to sit and walk, how to eat, clean up, drink our tea, care for the place that has been allotted to us, see who we truly are when the fluff is stripped away. We start from the beginning and do not jump ahead of ourselves. This is the time for meeting ourselves, when all covers and masks are taken away. In this simple manner, we grow to realize what it means to be alive, and also to live with another—what is needed in order to function in a way that is helpful to all participants. Like it or not, we learn how to live with our neighbors, those who are sitting on either side of our cushion.

BECOMING A GOOD NEIGHBOR

Just as everyone wants a good relationship, everyone wants a good neighbor on either side of him during sesshin. Who sits next to you can make a huge difference. Although you do not look at or speak to your neighbor for the entire length of sesshin, by the end of the retreat you know all there is to know about the person and often feel as close to her as if you had known her your entire life.

The neighbor can be a strong source of support, or a difficult hindrance. As the sittings go on day after day, it is impossible not to sense what that person is going through. If the person sits strongly, doesn't move, stays focused and does her best, her strength and bravery encourage and uphold you. However, if she becomes unsettled, shifts constantly, becomes messy, does not participate or misbehaves in countless other small ways, this can easily affect your sitting as well. Then, just as in any relationship, you can either let circumstances demoralize you, or you can decide to sit extra strongly, to become a source of strength for both of you.

In life we carry the illusion that we can choose our relationships, our partners or our neighbors at will. If we don't like them very much, if we're not getting the support we want from them, we can just get up and walk away. During sesshin we have no choice about who sits next to us. We must simply accept whoever is there. This itself is wonderful practice for living a life of love.

So much of the pain we encounter in life and in relationships is resistance to what we find on our plate. Most of our energy and attention goes into the struggle to make things different or better, or to change one partner for the next. When we stop resisting our neighbors or our partners, amazing things happen, enormous energy is freed up to love.

Penny couldn't bear sitting next to Thalia at sesshin. Thalia coughed, moved, sneezed and cried. As soon as Penny's zazen began going deeper, Thalia would do something to distract her. There were a million things Penny tried in the beginning to block her out. She pretended Thalia wasn't there at all. She focused with all her strength and even began singing songs in her head. It didn't matter. Thalia was planted there next to her for a full seven days. There was nothing she could do to avoid her. Part of the training during the sesshin is to learn how to live beside someone who makes you nuts. Not until you relax and accept the entire situation as it is, does your zazen go deeper and your partner calm down.

The way you react to the person beside you deeply affects her as well. If you struggle against her, hate her or blame her, her discomforting behavior usually intensifies. When you allow her to be just as she is, something can shift for both of you. As the famous saying goes:

> It is as if we change the whole course of life
> by changing our attitude towards it.
> —RALPH WALDO EMERSON

MAINTAINING OUR COMPOSURE

Learning to sit beside a difficult neighbor, no matter what she is doing, and maintain our own strength gives us the basis for all relationships. We learn how to be with our partners lovingly and constructively, no matter what they are going through. We do not take their upset personally, or enter into their world of pain. We become a source of support for them instead by maintaining our own strength and reality.

In relationships some become upset when their partner is out of sorts. They respond to anger with anger, to rejection with rejection, or take on their partner's concern as their own. But abnegating your own reality for the way your partner feels, in the erroneous belief that it will help the situation, is always a mistake.

If you stand firm and allow your partner to experience his own feelings, if you do not take anything personally, you are offering a gift to him. You are allowing your partner to have his own experience and your acceptance as well. When you don't take upset personally, he can more easily see its true source and also see other ways to respond. By not rejecting or blaming your partner for how he is feeling, you are offering unconditional love.

Emily, thirty-two, had been seeing Dave, who is forty, for four years. Their relationship was comfortable and had fallen into an expected pattern of routines. They'd visit his family for Thanksgiving, her family for Christmas. They went to the same restaurants for dinner and took the same two-week vacation every April in the Caribbean. Emily wondered if she had already experienced what life would be like with Dave, if there could ever be anything new and exciting in their relationship. She occasionally caught herself looking at younger men, fantasizing about exciting, different encounters, and wondered if she could deal with the monotony of being with Dave forever. On the other hand, she didn't know if she should just cut it all off, and have wasted the past four years of her life for no good reason.

It could be said that Emily was staying with Dave for practical reasons, largely based upon her desire for security and fear of losing valuable time. But her desire for other men indicates a yearning for the excitement she no longer found or allowed herself to have with Dave. Enmeshed in the secure routine they had established, Emily had not gone deeper in her experience of what it means to truly love. By leaving one partner for another, excitement and thrills may increase temporarily, but ultimately this pattern leads nowhere, except to an addiction to being excited and to developing a need for constant change.

GOING TO SESSHIN

As Emily's anguish about her relationship with Dave deepened, she started to practice Zen. She decided to attend a sesshin, hoping that this would bring about a radical change. We often go to sesshin wanting whatever it is that we are focusing upon in our lives at that time. Emily was longing for change in her relationship, and she hoped sesshin would propel her into it.

"I'm going because I can't change, I can't make a move in the relationship," she told the senior student who registered her. "Also, I can't wait for something to happen anymore. I've had it with waiting." Emily felt that she would speed things up by going for the week.

After she got there and became oriented to what the week would be like, she breathed deeply, initially relieved.

She felt certain this week would provide a turning point for the rest of her life. She would not come home the same person. She would be able to leave Dave on the spot.

We all have huge expectations that we expect to be fulfilled when we do something new. When we enter new relationships, we usually place these expectations onto the new relationship as well.

By the end of the first day of sesshin, Emily was exhausted, bored, achy and sad. Her legs hurt and her back was stiff. She couldn't believe that she would have to go through this same routine for seven days on end. She hadn't fully realized when she signed up what she was getting into.

None of us realize what we're getting into when we sign on for a relationship, either. At first it looks glamorous and exciting. Then the inexorable reality of everyday life begins to set in. Emily had no idea how she would get through a whole week. She wanted to talk it over with someone, but unless there was an emergency, unless someone was sick or needed something specific, talking was forbidden. She could not resolve her difficulty here by spilling it out on another.

Each person looked as though he was doing fine, Emily thought as she looked around. Was it only she who felt so irritated? She didn't have much time to ponder as lights were shut out half an hour after the schedule ended for the day. She lay there in her bed, tossing, desperately trying to fall asleep. She'd have to be up at four thirty the next morning.

WANTING EVERYTHING
TO GO OUR WAY

By the middle of the second day, Emily felt lonely and angry. When the meals were served, she refused her food. That will let them know something's wrong, Emily thought, trying to get attention of some kind. The student who served the food just passed her by, however, serving the person next to her. She was the one who would be hungry, she realized, if she did not take what was offered when it came. In like manner, she was the one who would stay miserable if all through sesshin she was determined to focus upon her own personal agenda, rather than focus upon her breath, which came and went regardless of everything, bringing new life each moment and taking old hurts away. But Emily just sat there thinking how she could get away.

By the end of the third day, Emily, unwilling to give up her thoughts and fantasies, decided to run away. There was no way she was going to continue like this. Day after day the same things happened. There was no change or release. She felt as if the whole world was on her shoulders. There was no one to help or to talk to. Except for brief meetings with the teacher, which were only about her zazen, she could not turn to anyone else. She had hoped this sesshin would expedite her life, that she would be through with waiting, but here there was nothing but waiting itself. She sat there waiting for the sitting to end—desperate for the bell to ring out. In a sense sesshin is a microscope, intensifying and enlarging both our way of functioning and the issues we are dealing with. As the days go by it becomes impossible not to see who we are and what we are up against. Hiding in denial and fantasy no longer becomes possible.

Emily's sense of what it meant to be fully alive was built upon change, excitement and rejection of boredom and of the daily routine. In sesshin, in order to survive, she had to completely enter into and embrace the routine itself. She had to forget about her personal agenda and be fully in each moment as it came. That was the only way for time to pass easily. That was the only way to discover moments of beauty and joy.

At the end of the third day, Emily packed her bags just before lights went out. Then when it was dark, she went out the back door to her car, which was parked on a hill, and ran away.

Once on the road home, a sense of loss and failure encircled her, a sense of not having gone through what was needed and having deserted the person sitting next to her. As Emily drove a little farther, she realized there was nowhere she could really run.

Then, in the middle of the night on a country road, she turned her car around and drove back, in time to be at sesshin for the early morning sitting. Except for one student, who looked at her oddly the next day at breakfast, she didn't think that anyone even realized that she had gone—and returned.

RUNNING AWAY AND RETURNING

At some point in the sesshin, almost all students feel they cannot go on. But no matter what happens, they go forward with their scheduled activities, keeping mindful through them, no matter how they feel. This itself is an enormous lesson, both in sesshin and in relationships. No matter how we feel, we do not act impulsively. We do not let our feelings dictate the next step to take. We just put one foot in front of the other and continue doing what needs to be done. We do not dwell upon our upset either, or assign some special meaning to it. If we do it becomes hard to continue.

As the days go by we cannot help but see that waves of feelings come and go, much like high and low tide at the ocean. Instead of getting pulled offshore by our passing fantasies and feelings, we simply return our attention to what we are doing, where the next step is taking us. As we do so over and over, the storms fade away and it becomes easier to also see clearly.

Of course there are those who run away from sesshin, just as there are those who run away from their lives (and relationships). As they pack up and slip out the back door, there may even be an initial sense of elation, jubilation. Out of there, finally! They may jump in their car and drive their car at breakneck speed down the hill, but then they suddenly realize there is nowhere they can really run. Wherever they go, they take themselves along.

Leaving is hard to do. Returning is even harder. Some do not return because they cannot face the shame of having left. But once an individual is able to return to a sesshin (or relationship), there is now the possibility of her making it her very own, fully appreciating its value and gaining some humility along the way. Some punish themselves for leaving. But the true focus should be upon the wonder and strength needed to come back again.

We return when we realize that there is nowhere to run to, that we must learn patience, persistence and the beauty of life's ordinary routines. We are then ready to understand relationships, the sameness we have to face with our partner day in and day out. Then we are ready to break through the veneer of boredom and find out what it means to really love.

STOPPING THE WAR

Drinking a cup of green tea, I stopped the war.
—PAUL REPS, IN *ZEN FLESH, ZEN BONES*

Those who leave sesshin and relationships do so because of the war that rages within. Conflicts, doubts and painful memories accost them constantly. Their lives are lived in a state of siege, with both others and themselves. When something arises that is discomforting, their first response is to fight, resist, escape. This is how they run their relationships as well.

Joseph came to sesshin because most of his relationships deteriorated into fighting matches. Little by little, he felt that the women he dated started to control him. He could feel it happening miles away. The minute he had the least little sign of it, the hairs on his neck bristled.

"It's happened so many times by now," Joseph said, "that I'm an expert in calling it quits. I let them know as soon as I can that they can't dominate me."

Joseph was an expert in testing women. He would subtly refuse do whatever they wanted and as soon as they became upset, he'd let them know that he was not someone who could be pushed around. Sooner or later the relationship ended.

Finally, in a desire to be rid of all relationships, Joseph became a Zen student. He wanted an end to the fighting he had grown to detest. In the beginning, his sitting on the cushion was a rejection not only of women, but of all relationships. He was turning his back, saying no to it all. It gave him a strange sense of victory. Who needed others? he thought. He would get his own needs met.

However, just because Joseph had turned his back didn't mean that the war within had stopped raging. His fights with different women, his wish not to be dominated, continued in his head. After sitting through the first several days of sesshin, he began to feel defeated again. Joseph sat with his own battle raging until the last day of sesshin when he was served a cup of green tea.

Joseph was exhausted, defeated and shamed when the time came to turn around on the cushion and receive a cup of green tea. Though it was the last thing he wanted to do, like the others he took his teacup from the place behind him, turned around and lifted his cup when the servers came. One placed a scoop of green powder in the cup, another poured hot water in and a third whisked the tea with a bamboo whisk.

As Joseph put the cup to his lips, his entire attention suddenly became absorbed in feeling the hot tea in his mouth. How delicious. How beautiful. Everything disappeared except the exquisite taste of the moment. Warm tears flooded his face as he was engulfed in gratitude. What in the world was there to fight about? What an idiot he'd been.

At that moment the battle within stopped raging. Joseph was able to receive the delicious tea. He was able to fully taste it and give thanks.

Rather than become gnarled up in battles with one another, how much better to be able to become still and see what we are receiving, taste it fully and say thank you. And how much better to see that the real root of our battles is most likely not with another, but with the dissatisfaction boiling within. If we don't see this at some point or another during sesshin and during life as well, it can be hard to go on.

DEVELOPING PERSISTENCE

In order to get to the point Jeff arrived at, persistence is vital. As the days pass during sesshin, endless reactions, fantasies, complaints, desires and old memories will arise. When we do not run away from them, we experience this inner cacophony that runs our lives. Some of it may be upsetting. Some of it may be enticing or beautiful. But whether what arises is pleasant or unpleasant, we learn to realize that all of it just comes and goes. This is just the scenery of our practice. It is not the essential road home.

Most relationships are fueled by this shifting inner panorama. Rather than being aware of what is driving us, we feel that the other person is the cause of our happiness, or will save us from our pain. Sometimes, in fact, relationships are nothing more than an effort to keep ourselves from being in touch with what is going on inside.

As the days pass at sesshin, as we sit without moving for so many hours, physical pain and discomfort come. Although we cannot move around to alleviate it, we become very surprised to realize that pain, too, will wax and wane. Like moments in relationships, one sitting can be painful, the next joyous. The more we persist, the easier it is to include it all. As we sit, without moving, through what might feel like unbearable pain, something amazing happens: the pain eventually vanishes, often transforming into pure joy.

Needless to say, the same can be true in relationships—just before we are ready to go to a deeper level, pain and fear often arise, causing many to run. If one can persist through these unwanted feelings, something truly beautiful may then have the chance to emerge. Sesshin is deep training in not running away but persisting through everything and simply doing what comes next. There is nothing more crucial than our ability to develop and endure in relationships, which the training in sesshin provides.

DOING WHAT NEEDS TO BE DONE NEXT

A student traveled far to see a great Zen master. Finally, he arrived at his hut. The master welcomed the student into his small, sparse dwelling and offered him a cup of tea. Eagerly, the student accepted. The master then slowly took a teapot, filled it with water and put it on the stove. Both the master and student then sat in silence, waiting for the water to boil. Finally, after what seemed like forever to the student, the tea was prepared. The master slowly brought one cup to the student and they sat together drinking their tea.

When he had finished, the student put his cup down.

"Did you drink all your tea?" the master asked.

"Yes."

"Fine. Now, wash your cup."

—FROM *ZEN FLESH, ZEN BONES,*
COMPILED BY PAUL REPS AND NYOGEN SENZAKI

There is a great tendency in all of us to stay where we have been, to play the past over and over in our minds, to refuse to let the moment pass. However, in relationships, rather than stay stuck dwelling upon the past, upon what should have happened or been said, it is crucial to stay in the present moment fully, and when that moment is over, immediately move on to the next.

The master in the story above showed great love to the student. He welcomed him into his hut, prepared the tea and had the student wait with him while it boiled. Then he even offered a crucial instruction: "After you drink your tea, wash your cup."

Do not leave traces behind you. When one activity is over, do what needs to be done next. After you have been served, take care of that which has served you. Do not overlook the cup. Be grateful for everything that is offered. Be mindful of how you receive it as well.

This is also a crucial instruction for relationships. The student had to wait while the tea was boiling until the proper moment came for the master to actually pour it, and then to drink. How many are able to wait in relationships until the proper moment for the next step? Often we push for something long before the other is ready, or we hesitate long past the time action is due. Sometimes we receive the tea (the person we are with) mindlessly, not really present or tasting it, just gulping down whatever is in our cup.

How many are then simply able to wash their teacup—do what comes next in the relationship, take care of what needs to be taken care of and leave no mess behind? Instead, many become fixated upon one part of the relationship and have no idea how to proceed, what step to take next. They hold on to resentments or refuse to move forward until their needs are met. But after you drink your tea, simply wash the cup. The best way to overcome resentments is to stay in the present and simply take the next action that is indicated, then take the next one after that. This breaks the hold of the past upon you and allows each moment to be new and fresh. No need either to wonder about how to do it. The place you are in will always show you what is needed. Try it and see.

TAKING YOUR WHOLE TEATIME

Sesshin teaches us to honor time, stop rushing, stay firmly planted in the moment and in what the moment requires of us. It teaches us not to run impulsively, but to focus upon our simple routines. If you learn to take your whole teatime to drink your cup of tea, you will then also be able to take all the time that is given to truly be with the person you are with. Whoever that may be. You will not be driven to escape him due to boredom, restlessness, fear, loneliness or whatever else arises from within. Instead, you will become a space in which a true relationship can begin.

In fact, it doesn't matter at all who the other person is. The ability to love and to be present is entirely up to you. Whoever is seated beside you, or whoever appears on your path, is part of the amazing manifestation of life. Why can't we accept and revere it? Why can't we offer all a beautifully prepared cup of tea?

Stepping-Stones to Love
Staying Where You Are

1. PERSISTENCE

What needs persistence in your life? Which relationships have you persisted in? Which have you cut short? Notice the difference between them and see what allows you to go on. How do you feel when you do that?

Today, pick a relationship that is almost in tatters and decide to persist. Keep your focus. Do whatever needs to be done to keep the door open. Do it no matter how you feel. Watch what happens then, to both of you.

2. JAZZING UP RELATIONSHIPS

What do you do to jazz up your relationships, to keep them from getting dull and boring? What kind of strain does this put on you and on the other person? Does it allow either of you to be real?

What happens if you stop doing this? Take a look and see. Is there some communication that needs to be made? Is there sadness between you or a sense of loss? Take time to share and explore this fully. Often jazzing up relationships is a sugar coating to cover up something missing or wrong. Sometimes it actually prevents something new from happening. Little by little, stop jazzing up one relationship. See what happens. Then do it with another. The energy restored to you will then be available for real movement and growth.

3. ENDING THE WAR

What's the fight you're having in relationships over and over again? Who are you really fighting with? What's at stake in this battle? If it's power and control you're after, what happens when you get that? Is your thirst satiated? Do you truly feel powerful and invulnerable, or is it a mirage? (Usually, the effort to dominate others leaves us more frail and nervous than when we began.) Also, what happens to the other person? Is it possible to be in love and share joy in a scenario like this?

Today, decide the war is over. Decide there's no battle to be won. What happens then? Are relationships suddenly boring and pointless? Can you persist through that sense of boredom and allow something new to open up?

4. ESCAPE

How much time do you spend escaping in relationships? (Either thinking about escaping or doing it silently.) What are the particular ways you escape? Do you listen with a smile on your face, but are really a thousand miles away? Do you silently dream about other people? Do you keep telling yourself this relationship is a stopgap measure?

What are you running from now? If you knew you had only a few days left on earth with this person, how would you be?

Take a long walk with the person you're with, letting go of distractions. Just be together as fully as you can. Focus on who is really there with you. Let him be who he is. Let your-

self be who you are as well. When you feel ready, reach out
and take his hand.

5. DO NOT GIVE UP ON A PERSON—DO NOT GIVE UP ON YOURSELF

When we give up on another, we are simultaneously giving
up on ourselves. This instruction comes from the Tibetan
Buddhist *lojong* teachings. It urges persistence, faith and the
ability to stay the course through all changes. It does not
mean never to leave a relationship, but rather not to discard
or reject someone in your heart. Also, it means not to discard and reject yourself.

Consider someone you may have given up on. What
form does it take? Simply remind yourself of the instruction
and stop doing it. Realize that this person contains everything within him, as do you. Growth, love and goodness are
possible for all. Do not give up on the person—see the best
for him and the best of him. Do the same for yourself.

> Year after year
>   The flowers appear alike....
> Year after year ...
>   Men are not the same.
> —ZENRIN LEWIS, *THE BOOK OF THE ZEN GROVE*

Chapter 10

STRUGGLING WITH YOUR KOAN
(working on problems)

Look for it in front of you
And suddenly it's behind you.
—ZENRIN LEWIS, *THE BOOK OF THE ZEN GROVE*

MOST OF US TURN EVERYTHING THAT HAPPENS, especially relationships, into a problem that has to be solved.
Soon each day becomes an obstacle course and we're constantly jumping through hoops. Some prefer to delay any
action until they have all the strategies and outcomes set.
They want to know exactly what they'll be up against before
they make a move. Similarly, there are those who won't venture out of familiar neighborhoods, routines or groups of
friends for fear of being taken by surprise. Being unprepared is the greatest nightmare these individuals can think
of. They dread not knowing the "right" response to make.

Being "wrong" turns into a disaster. Every action they take is filled with worry about the consequences.

The worry and fear these individuals go through can become especially paralyzing in matters of love, and they quickly turn relationships into the supreme problem of their lives. After all, there is the greatest possibility of failure in relationships, and also the greatest possible prize: love.

But approaching life as if it were something to be conquered or vanquished does not lead to a life of love, it leads only to safety. Love is not safe, nor is it the outcome of strategies adopted by the rational mind. Love takes us by surprise, when we are open and ready for it. Preparing for falling in love requires an entirely different approach. We must discover a new way of being with problems. As we do this we can even discover that, in fact, there are no problems, there are just the *koans* life constantly presents.

An essential part of Zen training is knowing what a koan is, being ready to receive it and, when one has been given a koan, learning how to solve it. The work of solving koans is actually training in the art of learning how to fall in love.

In every relationship there are problems that seem insoluble that cause feelings of confusion and helplessness on both sides. Each party struggles to convince her partner of the validity of her point of view and often the debate ends in deadlock. These problems may even turn into obsessions, causing individuals to reenact the same confrontation endlessly, to no avail. Soon they exhaust themselves, and when this process has gone on for as long as they can bear, the relationship is over. (Being caught in this quagmire is a major cause of relationships ending.) Not until individuals know how to relate to their insoluble problems can their relationships really flourish and love have a chance to grow.

WORKING ON A KOAN: A ZENDO LESSON

When a Zen student reaches a sufficient point of maturity in his practice, he receives a koan from the Zen master. A koan is a seemingly insoluble problem or riddle, such as *Listen to the sound of one hand clapping* or *Show me your original face before your parents were born*. Koans defy logical understanding. They cannot be penetrated by the rational mind, will not be answered by formulas or slogans. The more we try to think them through, the farther we are from the mark. Yet an answer must be brought to the master. It is said in the zendo that unless one solves the koan or penetrates the essence of his life, he has missed a great opportunity and may never know who he really is.

As she takes up her koan, naturally the student fails again and again. Just as in relationships, she then often feels stupid, frustrated and ashamed. More than that, she feels as if there is no answer to the bind she is in.

But part of the process of solving one's koan is learning how to work on it, learning how to allow the solution to find us. Everyone endures feelings of shame and stupidity before allowing his usual way of confronting the world to subside.

In order to pass our koan (in order to learn to deal with insoluble problems in life and relationships), we must take a radical step—we must overturn the very way in which we know our world and see through our conditioning.

Our usual way of knowing what is right is based upon what our rational mind and external senses tell us. We observe, measure and define in order to gain mastery and control. We feel that by thus molding the world, we are powerful, strong and in command.

But in fact we spend most of our lives searching outside ourselves for things we already know. Running headlong toward various disciplines such as psychology, theology and sociology, we hope that someone else will provide answers and authority in our lives. We turn to priests, rabbis and psychoanalysts in order to understand life more deeply. Without doing this we consider ourselves entirely blind. And in one sense it is so.

Scientific and objective knowledge has its function and great usefulness, but it cannot bring healing into a torn relationship; it cannot restore one's faith in love.

Where science ends, love begins. Love cannot be known through observation, as it has no form. Although we can prolong a relationship, we cannot gain mastery or control over the love that joins us together. In order to gain assurance and understanding in this realm, in order to answer the koans life presents, we must stop our search for answers in the logical world.

Instead we turn to our own deep experience, which will lead us not to *know* more, but to *be* more. We do not use only our brain, but our entire being. This can show us how to walk into a relationship and provide strength, simplicity and beauty. This inner knowing tells us that despite our so-called insoluble problems, all is well.

In order to touch this within ourselves it is necessary to ask new kinds of questions, to view events in our lives with different eyes. We do not try to mold or control our experience, nor do we explain it away. Instead we simply meet with it, become acquainted, then we let it instruct us and be our guide.

TAKING THE PATH OF HUMILITY

In one sense, we are describing the path of humility. It requires the strength to let go of our need to control ourselves and our world and to recognize that indeed we are not the most powerful; there is something larger than us, and we must simply learn how to connect with this in order to find our true answers.

Plato said that we are born knowing everything and that our lives simply consist of the process of forgetting. We have forgotten where we came from and where we are going. We have forgotten our purpose here on this beautiful earth.

Now, working with our koans, we simply remember the knowledge that was always ours.

In a time of crisis, pain and sadness, it is of the utmost urgency to learn how to reconnect with our own inner source of wisdom and strength. Koans give us the opportunity. They are designed as mirrors to see into ourselves.

Diana, twenty-six, had been dating Jason for one year and was very happy—most of the time. But problems kept coming up as they got to know each other more deeply: differences in viewpoints, different ideas about whom to vote for, how money should be spent, about where they would live, about how many kids they would have and how they would raise them. Deep down though, they both loved each other very much, and Diana felt that their love for each other could overcome anything. But was she fooling herself? Was the relationship worth all the effort? Would the problem solving ever end?

Some say that Diana simply fell in love with the wrong person and entered into a situation fraught with ongoing conflict. Others would argue that she lacked sufficient flexibility to live with and learn from a partner with whom she had natural differences. She could choose a partner whose point of view was closer to hers, but then again her love for Jason could force her to grow, develop new parts of herself and ultimately discover entirely new ways of living. Which road should she take? She couldn't decide. Her conflict seemed to have no solution. Little by little it was eroding their love.

WHO IS ASKING ME THAT?

By the time Diana started Zen practice, her obsession with Jason intensified, interfering with her ability to sleep. She could neither hold on to him nor let him go. Even during zazen her relationship with him was continually on her mind.

At her special request, she was given an interview with the Zen master. Diana was excited about this. She had seen the Zen master several times in the zendo, and was impressed. He walked with such an air of certainty, spoke with such authority that she knew she was in good hands. He would see the situation for what it was.

During the interview the Zen master offered her a cup of tea. Even in the midst of drinking her tea, Diana began speaking hurriedly, pouring out all the details of her problem and how no solution could be found. The Zen master placed his teacup down on the table firmly and said, "Who is asking me this?"

Who is asking me this is a koan. Who is the one bringing this problem to me? Why is it a problem? He turned the situation entirely around. Rather than dwell upon the specifics of her situation, Diana was to simply dwell upon who was asking this question of him.

Diana immediately became silent.

"Well?" he grunted, waiting for a reply.

"I don't know," she said lamely.

"Then find out!"

He got up swiftly, and left.

Diana sat there, dumbfounded.

If we don't know *who* is asking the question—*who* disagrees with her boyfriend, *who* is seeking the answer—we can never find our way out.

As Diana worked on her koan, her obsession with her boyfriend began to die down. Her attention was focused elsewhere, upon the very source of her experience. It didn't seem to matter to Diana so much any longer whether Jason liked this or that, or how he viewed different issues. There was room for him to be who he was, and room for her to have her own views as well. When he tried to engage her in their usual struggles about which point of view to adopt, Diana couldn't get absorbed in the struggle, as she used to do. Instead, she listened to him carefully. Just listened. It felt wonderful to be just listening, not having to necessarily have an answer or tie everything up.

"Well, what will we do if we disagree on child rearing when we marry—if we do?" Jason persisted in his anxiety.

"We'll know when we get there," Diana said simply. "When the situation comes up, we'll see what it is."

Diana did not need to project into the future about what would or would not happen with Jason, but had enough self-trust so that she could allow life to bring what it did. She would be able to respond to it when it came.

KNOWING WHAT TO DO
WHEN WE GET THERE

So many of our worries, complaints, "problems" and struggles revolve around how we will handle some situation projected in the future. It is impossible to fall and stay in love when this kind of concern occupies our mind. We are not then present or available to the moment, but are entwined in some fantasy that has gripped our mind.

The truth is that most of what we are projecting does not come to pass anyhow. Something else happens. And when it happens, if it does, we are an entirely different person then, with different resources to handle it with. The situation can appear very different to us at that time.

Most of the problems we grapple with are simply created in our minds. They do not exist. And if they did, they could usually be handled naturally, in an instant. When we place all faith and attention in our obsessive mind, we can be assured we will live with one insoluble problem after the next. When we place our faith and attention in our deepest selves, in our zazen, solutions arise plentifully. They arise when needed. When we get there we know what to do.

THE NATURE OF OBSESSION

Most of the time when we think we are working on "problems" we are simply allowing ourselves to obsesses over them. We run the same loop of ideas through our minds repeatedly, never allowing in any fresh air. Somehow we believe there is only one solution and that solution is right, others are wrong. If we attempt to consider the problem from a different angle, the obsessive mind warns us not to do this—it is a matter of life and death.

Obsessive thinking deprives us of hope and distorts reality, causing confusion and limitation and allowing manipulation of our minds. It is therefore exceedingly important to realize what we are up against when we undertake our koans, when we struggle to solve impenetrable problems in our relationships. We are facing all that has limited and confined us, causing us to live a life of problems and suffering rather than a life of love.

Koans dissolve obsessive thinking because when we work on our koan we do not "think" about it rationally. Our rational minds will never find the answer. Instead, when we work on our koan, some say we should sit on it, like a mother hen sitting on eggs in her nest. In order to solve the koan we must move into another part of our being, the part that knows life directly and reacts in a clear, spontaneous way. The answer we receive is a new form of communication, one that bypasses the confusion and distortion created by the rational mind.

DISSOLVING MIXED MESSAGES

The mixed messages we constantly receive from others and from ourselves fuel obsessive thought and keep relationships turbulent as well. Mixed messages are when people say one thing and do another, present themselves in one way and then behave as someone else. Not knowing which message to respond to, an individual facing this becomes paralyzed, unable to choose or act appropriately.

This has also been called mystification. It describes the conscious or unconscious efforts of one person to misdirect or deny the feelings and perceptions of another. The individual doing it feels ambivalent and tries to cope with two opposing feelings at once. He may love and hate his partner simultaneously. He may want her to come closer and also to go away. He then communicates these opposing feelings simultaneously and his partner has no idea which message to listen to or believe. So many say, "I know he loves me, and yet he does everything he can to sabotage the relationship. One minute he's coming closer, the next minute he's running away." This kind of confusion tears relationships apart. As soon as it starts happening in a relationship, warning bells should go off.

Such confusing communication is quite common in relationships and its consequences must be understood. The person receiving these conflicting messages often feels as if she doesn't have any solid ground to stand on, because she doesn't know which message to respond to. Before long she starts to feel she is being driven crazy. And she is. To live a life of love and sanity, we must know where we stand and what is wanted of us, and be able to respond directly to the messages we receive.

Unlike confusing communication in a relationship, the answer to a koan is always straightforward. Like a baby chick bursting out of its shell, the answer reveals itself directly, bypassing fantasy and obsession, all the lies we tell and receive. As we work on our koans, we are tackling the very essence of the confused mind itself.

When Sara came to the zendo, she was caught in a whirl of mixed messages, and her attempt to solve them had developed into an obsession with her boyfriend.

"I keep trying to figure out what's true and what isn't," she said, distraught. "I don't know if he loves me or not. He keeps saying he loves me, but I don't feel it. He constantly makes odd comments about me and no matter what he says I feel that he basically looks down on me. The longer we're together the worse I feel about myself. Every time he comes into the room I wonder if I'll make the grade this time. He tells me I'm going crazy. There's not a bit of truth to what I feel—he is absolutely in love."

FINDING OUR OWN COMPASS

Sara had lost her compass. She didn't know which messages to listen to and which to ignore. As the relationship went on, she began to feel as if she were on trial every time he came into the room. Was there something else he would find wrong today?

Rather than respect and act upon the way she was feeling, Sara began think she was crazy. She went into agreement with her boyfriend, still desperately wanting him to see her point of view as well. She would give him examples of ways he behaved that made her feel bad, like standing her up for dates, not calling when he said he would or speaking ill about her before others, but no matter what she said, he discounted it and looked baffled. "All of that amounts to nothing. I told you I love you," is all he would say.

Even during zazen, Sara kept rolling these conflicting realities around in her mind. Which one of us is right? she pondered. If he loves me so much, why do I feel so lousy? Is it possible I'm not able to receive love? One of us must be crazy. How can I find out who?

Sara must learn to accept her own feelings, perceptions and experiences, though they may differ from those of her partner, and even from those of others in her world. She must learn to validate her own intuitive being. In order to solve a koan, we must radically know and accept the one who lives within.

DISCOVERING THE RIGHT ANSWER

When most people start to work on their koans, they, too, believe there is one right answer and if they don't find it, they are going to fail. Similarly, many feel there is only one right mate for them in life and if they lose this one person, they'll never find another again. Love becomes a matter of succeeding or failing, being validated by another or not.

When working on their koans, these individuals spend endless time trying to get the right answer so the Zen master will approve. Fortunately, however, in Zen practice, the more a student does this, the more the Zen master says no. Pleasing another, looking for validation, taking on another's reality is never the answer to the koan of life. It is never the way to live a life of love.

The very process of working on koans teaches us how to stop this behavior. It shows us that there can be many right answers, that we cannot fail as long as we are practicing and that the very act of bringing an answer is success itself. And beyond that, if we simply continue, sooner or later a real answer must emerge. It cannot be any other way. Working on koans also shows us that the final authority resides within ourselves.

The same is true in relationships. It is impossible to fail if we extend love. Whether or not the person accepts it is incidental. Our ability to love is what makes the difference. As we are able to fully acknowledge and accept ourselves, no matter what the person's reaction, we become simultaneously able to accept and acknowledge him just as he is.

Fear, confusion and manipulation never give rise to love. They give rise to attachment, dependency and possessiveness, the counterfeit coins many live with. By viewing relationships as koans, as chances to be straightforward, unique and clear, we open the door for all the strength and happiness that a loving relationship is ready to bring.

As Sara's practice deepened, rather than listen to her boyfriend's proclamations or focus upon his covert behavior, she became absorbed in the experience of being in the present, simply watching, listening and becoming aware of all that was presented to her. Rather than focus upon the external world, she focused upon the one who was perceiving it within.

"What he did or did not do, what he said or did not say, began to have less effect upon me," said Sara. "I was becoming grounded in myself. I was getting a sense of where I was standing, who I was, and became less hungry for his approval. I began to see his behavior as a reflection of his mind. Soon the relationship simply faded. He couldn't tolerate the fact that I wasn't upset. To him it meant I didn't love him. I, in turn, saw all of this as a crazy kind of dance. It wasn't so hard to step off the dance floor when I saw what was entailed."

Sara had been able to find a new ground of being, a different way of perceiving what went on in their relationship.

While rooted in her own truth, she did not get caught up in fantasies that had no basis and no hope. Now she had found the freedom to stay and the freedom to go.

SEEING WHOSE REALITY IT IS

Lack of trust in one's own reality poses a greater danger than being right or wrong, or deciding who is or isn't crazy. The lack of trust in one's reality is the cause of endless suffering, indecision and loss of self-esteem. We can never solve a koan or have a wonderful relationship until we have faith in our own inner selves.

So many say, "I don't know what happened, but as my relationship went on, I felt as though I was disappearing. The person I was at the beginning turned into someone else, someone I could barely recognize. I don't know how this happened but slowly I became the person my boyfriend wanted me to be. After the relationship ended I was entirely lost. Now I'm afraid to enter a relationship again."

Lack of knowing and trusting oneself causes many to disappear in relationships or to become someone they don't recognize. Some acquiesce to the reality of their partner, to keep him happy or to keep things from falling apart. This is the price they feel they need to pay in order to be loved. But this price is enormous. It has nothing to do with love. When we give up our reality, we are giving up our very selves. How can we love and receive love from another if we are not there? When we are in a truly loving relationship, we receive the gift of being known and accepted. We become more, not less, of who we are. We receive the space in which to bloom. This is how we know we are in a loving relationship. We are blooming, and the one we love is blooming as well.

> We are all flowers blooming in a blooming universe.
> —SOEN ROSHI

In order to bloom, in order to solve our koan, we must learn to value and validate our own inner knowing, to live our own truth and no one else's.

Stepping-Stones to Love
Solving Our Problems

I. YOUR KOAN

What koan are you grappling with daily, though you may not have thought of it that way before? What keeps your happiness from you, keeps you going in circles trying to figure it out? Spend time noticing. Perhaps you have more than one koan? Perhaps there is one you've had from childhood? Start by identifying this as a koan, and stop trying to figure it out.

2. WORKING ON THE KOAN

How do you work on your koans? Notice the thoughts, actions and hopes that continually appear in your life. Notice your usual solutions to the issues that trouble you. Pay attention to the repetitive quality of them. Now, also notice what results you get. What is the effect of the solutions you choose upon your life?

For now, be willing to stop working on your koan that way. Be willing to drop your old efforts. (The more effort we expend in the wrong direction, the more difficult the koan becomes.)

3. GREETING YOUR KOAN

Today would you be willing to greet your koan (your problem) as if it were an old, dear friend? Welcome it into your life. Do nothing more than that now. Spend time with it quietly, as you would just being with a dear friend. You wouldn't try to figure out your friend or change her, you would just enjoy her company. Remember, don't try to find a solution There is nothing to solve. Right now you are just spending quality time with your koan, enjoying its company.

4. ALLOWING YOUR KOAN TO SPEAK

Rather than dictate to your koan how it should be worked out, just allow *it* to speak to you. Listen to it totally. Your koan (or problem) is there because it has wisdom to provide. It may be asking something of you. It may have direction for the rest of your life. Just sit there listening, with no preconceptions. Listen with your complete body and mind. Allow the jewel of the koan, its purpose and message, to become completely clear.

5. MAKING A REPLY

Once we have understood our koan (our problem or relationship), some of us want to reply. It may be some new action, expression or decision—it varies every time. Be open to how you want to reply to your koan. Then do it, as soon as you can.

> When you become you,
> Zen becomes Zen.
> When you become you,
> The whole world falls in love.
> —ESHIN

Chapter 11

DOKUSAN: MEETING WITH THE MASTER
(moments of dramatic choice)

*If you don't go into the Tiger's Cave,
How can you get a Tiger Cub?*
— *THE BLUE CLIFF RECORD*

THERE ARE CRUCIAL MOMENTS in our lives when a dramatic situation presents itself and we must respond instantly. A vital choice must be made. The way in which we respond can change the course of our lives or the life of someone we love. There is no time to think. Action is required. (Not acting in these instances is action as well.) The sum of who we are and what we believe, value and desire will reveal itself by what we do.

Faced with a moment of truth, many individuals are struck dumb. Some let the moment pass them by, others become angry, try to stop it or say something they spend the rest of their lives regretting. But there is no way to change or fix a moment that has passed. This moment is an opportunity that comes and then departs, unable to be recaptured. One may call it a test or a point of destiny. Whatever we call it, this moment calls forth the essence of who we are, where we have developed and where we still have to grow.

Although moments like these seem comparatively rare, they happen more than we realize in both our lives and our relationships. Some people do not even realize that these opportunities are presenting themselves. They drift through life in such a haze that they are blind to what could be possible. Others become paralyzed by the sudden action demanded of them. The essence of Zen training is to make us so awake and spontaneous that when moments like these arise we are ready: we respond with our whole selves naturally.

When we lose an important relationship, either due to problems, illness or sudden change, it is natural to think about what else we could have done or said that would have made a difference. Many blame themselves and feel there was something they left undone. If they had only done just one more thing, or responded just a little differently, the outcome might have changed. As they dwell upon this, individuals often develop a sense of fear about the speed of time. They wish that time could go backward and allow them to replay the situation once again.

Usually we expect that life will go on forever, that others

will always be there for us. If things do not go well this time, we can always try again. This is not the mind of Zen training, where every second, every person, every encounter counts.

In Zen practice we learn how to live on the sharp edge of the moment, to become completely present so we can capture the moment and respond maximally. The idea is to respond from all of our being, doing exactly what is needed and required, though we could not have figured it out a second before. To live with this kind of dynamism makes the whole world come alive.

DOKUSAN: A ZENDO LESSON

Time is an arrow.

—ZEN SAYING

There is another element of Zen practice that prepares us for moments of dramatic choice. During Zen training the student goes for what is called *dokusan* (or *daisan*), a personal meeting with the master. This is an intense moment in training, and in many zendos, the students must run at full speed if they are to get a spot in line in time to meet with him.

Time is of the utmost importance. There is urgency not to let a second slip by. And beyond that, if you do not get to see the master this time around, who knows if you will again?

Some don't go to dokusan at all for a number of years (just as some don't get anywhere near intimacy in relationships). Others have to be pulled and prodded. There are those who love going and run there every chance they can get. Some haven't answered their koan, have nothing really to show the master, but continue to appear. Others go wanting the master to pass them—to say they are all right. Others enjoy frustrating the master by the confusion and sorrow they constantly present. Some may long for closeness with the master, or feel he'll provide a hint of some kind.

Needless to say, whenever we go to meet the master in dokusan (a process that can go on for many years), we bring with us exactly who we are right at that moment. We think we are bringing an answer to our koan, or showing the master what our practice is—and we are, because what we are bringing is simply ourselves. Nothing extra. Nothing left out. In dokusan there is nowhere to hide.

When the student arrives on the dokusan line, she will find herself sitting in a row, one behind the other, doing zazen, while awaiting her turn to go meet the master. The student in the front of the row rings the bell when her turn comes, to announce that she's coming. Then she rushes into the master's room, where he is waiting to receive her.

When the student goes into the master's chambers, she bows and then sits across from him in zazen. This meeting often lasts only a few moments and is not for the purpose of social exchange. In this meeting all is open and exposed— who you are and who you are not. Sometimes the master will pass the time entirely in silence. Often the student will be asked to present an answer to her koan, to show the master what she has attained. The master will listen, sometimes respond and sometimes not. Then he will ring his bell the moment the dokusan is over. In the early years of practice, the student may wonder if she passed or failed.

ENCOUNTERING MOMENTS OF SUDDEN DECISION

Amy, twenty-four, had been dating Steve since high school. She loved him very much, although sometimes she wondered if this was because he was so familiar. He was the only boyfriend she'd ever had, and she wondered if she was making a mistake in having spent so many years with him, not seeing who else was out there for her. One night, after dinner out, he surprised her by proposing. She felt torn by all of her conflicting feelings and had no idea what to say. She told him she would need to think it over. Hurt and baffled, Steve broke up with her the next morning. Amy was shocked and devastated. She felt that the best years of her life were behind her. Would she ever meet someone else? Had she made the wrong choice?

This was a situation in which Amy had to respond instantly, and present her full self. But Amy's full self wasn't available in her relationship. Doubts, conflicts and other expectations had robbed her energy and caused her to distrust both herself and the man she loved. When time came to declare herself, she was not able to act. Many lives are lived in this same state of paralysis.

No matter how much Amy agonized, there was nothing further she could do. Though she telephoned Steve and begged for the opportunity to discuss it further, he said there was nothing more to say. They'd been together so long, he felt that if she couldn't say yes in that moment, that told him all he needed to know.

It could be said that Amy hadn't had sufficient time to meet other men, know more about herself as a woman or be secure with the choice she was about to make. She might also have had issues about marriage and commitment. The fact that Steve could not allow her to take her time reflected poorly on him. Clearly, he, too, had conflicting feelings if he was ready to end the relationship abruptly.

Friends encouraged Amy to grieve over the relationship with Steve, date other men and go forward to build a new life. Amy had difficulty accepting this guidance. She could not get over the fact that she had lost the relationship in that one, crucial moment. Day after day she wondered how she could have responded in a way that would not have shut the door in her face.

When Amy went for her first dokusan, she sat on the line, waiting and trembling. She was exhausted after sitting so many hours up to then. Others sped by her as she got up from her cushion and rushed to the line. She wondered how they got up so quickly and where they were flying to. When she arrived in the place where others sat waiting, she got a seat at the end of the line. After ringing the bell and rushing to see the master, each student seemed to stay in the dokusan room for only a few moments. Some stayed longer. Amy had no idea why. After he was finished with each student, the master rang his bell announcing it was time for the next one to come.

Amy had no idea exactly what she would say when she came before him. She'd been a student for several months and hadn't received a koan. She simply sat, paying attention to her breath. A dull, ordinary practice, she thought, wondering how she could make herself interesting to him.

By the time Amy got to the beginning of the line and took the seat in front of the bell, it was late, almost the end of morning sitting, and time for lunch. Just as she took the stick to ring the bell announcing that she was coming, the student in charge of the line took the stick from her and rang the bell many times to announce that dokusan was over.

"Time is up," the student whispered to Amy.

Amy was shocked.

"Try again next time."

Amy went back downstairs into the zendo with the others, crestfallen. She couldn't believe she hadn't gotten in. She had waited and waited and nothing happened. Sitting downstairs in the zendo now, she began to cry.

Amy hadn't been present to the sharp edge of the moment. Her intention had not been high. She had gone along with how she was feeling, rather than realize that precious moments were coming. If she was not ready for them, present to them and willing to exert herself greatly, the opportunity would pass her by. Actually, Amy had lived her whole life this way. It was time for her to see what was going on.

TAKING EVERYTHING FOR GRANTED

Most of us do not ascribe sufficient importance to anything, let alone relationships. We go along any way we like, for as long as we wish, and take our lives together for granted. It always seems as if the moment of choice, the key encounter or the inevitable confrontation will happen sometime far down the road. Or perhaps we'll get by without it happening at all. Maybe our relationship can become a place to hide in, receive comfort, and no ultimate demand will be made of us. That was the attitude Amy brought to her time with Steve. It was also the attitude she brought to the zendo and the way she approached the dokusan line, ambling there halfheartedly.

Some rush to dokusan, weaving in front of others, not letting anybody get in their way. These are the students who demand perfection of everyone, including themselves. No matter what answer they present, however, the master will refuse. An overly frantic approach is not living on the sharp edge of the moment either.

These students wonder what they're doing wrong. Most try harder. The harder they try the more the master refuses.

After this goes on for a long while (years in some cases), these students feel like complete failures and run out of answers to present. They no longer run so quickly. This is a wonderful moment, because in order to enter Zen mind, one must go beyond right and wrong, failure and success.

So much of our lives is lived worrying if we are a failure or a success, especially in relationships. When we don't give the "right" answer, or get the response we crave from another, when we feel rejected and tossed out, many of us deem ourselves failures—and deem our relationships to be failures as well. This is one of the main causes of suffering in relationships, and why many individuals refuse to get up and try again. Or why they try to push their way in front of others, demanding that they be approved.

Neither of these responses works in dokusan, however. When we go to dokusan, when we have this intense, immediate, no-holds-barred encounter with the master, we are learning many things. Most of all we are learning about the basis of all relationships, and what is essential in order to really be with another and available for love.

When we go to see the master, just as when we enter relationships, it is crucial to be aware of how we are going. Are we bringing someone real to the encounter, or are we presenting a dream figure, a role we are playing, the shadow of who we really are? Do we go entirely focused upon the master, wanting his praise? Are we going hoping to get the answer right this time instead of failing again?

Having a true meeting with the master, or being able to

fall in love, never has anything to do with being a failure or a success. That notion must be completely discarded. In true dokusan there is no such thing. Success and failure are the world of the marketplace, the world of gain and loss. Instead, the Zen master will instruct the students to "come naked before me."

COME NAKED BEFORE ME

We create a mask to meet the masks of others. Then we wonder why we cannot love, and why we feel so alone.
—ESHIN

The Zen master is instructing students to remove the acquired ideas, conditioning, fears and games they have lived with their whole life long. If they come to dokusan wearing a mask, nothing real can happen.

Can one mask love another? Does a mask know how to communicate? Everything the mask says and does is for the purpose of hiding. But true communication is for the purpose of love. Each time we go to dokusan the implied question we are facing is: How much of your mask are you willing to relinquish? How much fresh air will you let into your life?

Throughout our lives we all play a variety of games. We help others keep their pretenses up and they help us keep ours. In one way this makes us feel safe and secure. In another it robs our true life, and allows us to live in a make-believe world where we become cardboard people, basically unreal. If someone knocks on our door to visit, there is no one home.

"Come naked before me" points to another way of relating. Here the true person is fully exposed and has a chance to speak and enter into dialogue. Here we are opening ourselves to something *other*. This situation is unpredictable and we may feel as if something dangerous is about to happen. But under these conditions a real meeting can take place.

REAL MEETINGS

What is a real meeting? What are we doing in dokusan with the Zen master? We are there to experience oneness, our connection with our true selves. We are there to be brave enough to allow our heart to speak out all by itself.

Our hearts have a language of their own. The voice of the heart is always eager to be heard, though we usually try to keep it stifled. Sometimes it simply bursts forth. Then a real meeting can take place.

A real meeting takes us home to our center. We do not feel alone. Our sense of alienation vanishes. We see that we are all truly one.

Real meetings can happen spontaneously. They can happen for a moment, or can last a while. They can happen between two people, or between a person and the sky. We cannot demand that a real meeting happen. But we can learn how to invite it in.

The most important components are two people who are real. This means that each person is willing to let go of his need to control the other or use the other for his selfish ends. They forget about wanting to see praise in the other's eyes, or needing to be important. They are not using the relationship as personal fantasy. They are simply willing to allow anything to happen, exactly as it wants to. They have forgotten about fear and protecting themselves. They may even see that there is nothing to protect.

This kind of meeting is tremendously liberating. When it happens, some begin to laugh out loud or even cry. Some say preparing for a meeting of this kind of like preparing to meet with a great king.

The dokusan room invites a meeting of this kind. World upon world can open up. And the limitless love we all consist of is released from our constricted hearts.

Stepping-Stones to Love Direct Encounters

1. THE EDGE OF THE MOMENT

What is of the greatest urgency to you? What matters most? What would you not put off doing? Is there a relationship in which you would not hesitate to do all that is required of you? What is it about this particular relationship that makes you feel this way? What about other relationships in which this is not so—what is the difference between them?

2. FAILURE AND SUCCESS

Where do you feel you fail in relationships? Where do you feel you succeed? Where do you feel others fail you? Where do they succeed? Take note of this carefully. Now, for today, let go of the idea of failure and success. Stop placing that judgment upon your relationships. See your relationships as perfect, no matter what happened, no matter what did or did not go as you wished. Try this and see what happens. Make a list of relationships that were important to you, and see every aspect of them as perfect, including yourself and your partner. How do you feel now about going forward in relationships and trying something new?

No matter what happened, the way in which we view our relationships is entirely up to us. No one has the power to spoil them for us. No one can make them beautiful. What choice are you making now?

3. TAKING OFF YOUR MASKS

Notice what masks and costumes you wear in your relationships. Notice what games you continue to play. Do not judge it as good or bad, just take a good look. Now become aware of the outcomes of these relationships. Are they fulfilling to you? Do they provide the nourishment you are hungering for? Can one mask love another? Is it even possible?

Take off one mask the next time you are with someone
special. Then take off a costume. See who you are straining
to be, what pretense you have to keep up. Just let it go, the
way we take off an old worn-out shoe. Give yourself the
pleasure of being no one special, and not needing your partner to be someone special as well.

4. REAL MEETINGS

Are you open to having a real meeting? Has this ever happened to you? Spend quiet time preparing, clearing the
space, inviting it in. (Different people prepare in a variety of
ways. Find the one that's best for you.) You can prepare by
meditating, walking in nature, going to the beach, painting,
singing or writing poems. You can prepare by clearing your
mind of old ways of being, and requesting something new
come to you, a larger experience of yourself and the universe. You can prepare by giving up fear and sorrow, saying
good-bye to loneliness, forgetting about judging yourself
and others. Or, if you have the heart for it, you can prepare
by going to the zendo, staying there and practicing until finally, one day, you are ready to run to dokusan.

> When you meet a master in the street,
> do not speak, do not be silent.
> Then how will you greet him?
> —FROM *ZEN FLESH, ZEN BONES,*
> COMPILED BY PAUL REPS AND NYOGEN SENZAKI

Chapter 12

ONE BREATH
(no separation)

Human happiness comes from perfect harmony with others.
—CHUANG-TZU

ALTHOUGH ALL OF US SAY WE WANT TO FIND LOVE, most of us spend the bulk of our time creating separation between ourselves and others. Once in relationships, it's easy to find things wrong with the other, focus on needs that are not being met or feel that too much is being asked of us. We feel safer and more natural when we declare our territory, make firm boundaries and feel that the needs and interests of others are basically different from our own. Many enjoy having opponents or enemies, and are at a loss when they do not. They know themselves in opposition to others and find it exciting to test their strength, enter competitions, come out on top and assert their superiority and dominance. This, in fact, can become their main source of identity.

A great deal of our upbringing encourages this. We are taught to compare ourselves to others, get the best in a deal, win at competitions and above all, not be made a fool of or become someone others will have a good laugh at.

A great deal of what is called relationship training consists of learning how to "succeed" in manipulating others to get them to do what we want, or influence and control the interaction. Finding someone to settle down with is like getting a good deal on an automobile. The person becomes a commodity. His value is determined by what he can deliver, how he ranks in the marketplace and how long the value will hold up. Men who leave marriages at midlife, when the children are grown and the wife is getting older, starting to wear down, are looking for someone who can boost their value in their own eyes and in the marketplace.

When you view people as commodities it is impossible to live a life of being in love. In fact, falling in love may be considered the most useless, foolish and even risky business one can undertake. One becomes vulnerable, childlike, innocent, happy and does not even bother manipulating those around her. There is no need to. One has all one wants. A life of love is a life of trust, service and happiness.

However, there are various fears that prevent us from giving up old ways. Some fear that once they give up their wariness or stop seeing the other as an opponent they will become swallowed up. There will be no hope of maintaining a separate identity, as they will be constantly succumbing to the wishes of the other. Love then becomes the ultimate dependency, taking their power away. These individuals see love as debilitating, not as providing autonomy and strength.

Fearing the loss of one's separate identity is based upon a wrong understanding of what true oneness is and what it means to be of service and to love.

ONE BREATH: A ZENDO LESSON

Relinquishing control is the way to invite love not only into our relationships, but into every moment of our lives. When we let go of divisiveness and return to our source and rest there, then we cannot help but be filled with a sense of that which is boundless and available to all. The love that emanates from our source is available to all who call upon it; others cannot take it away because it is our essential nature, who we truly are. As we return to the "one breath" in the zendo, we realize that we are not sustained and replenished by others. We are replenished by returning to our source.

In the zendo, each person sits besides the other, and focuses upon his own breath. But whom does this breath belong to? The breath that one person breathes out, his neighbor breathes in. This breath is freely given and freely received. If for even one moment we didn't receive breath, or weren't willing to give it back, our life would be over. The act of breathing is the substratum of our lives. Falling in love is no different. We breathe it in and out with every breath we take. In order to breathe, we must trust that our next breath will always be there. In order to love, we must trust that love is abundantly available and can never be taken away.

As the students sit together and breathe, little by little the question naturally arises: Who is breathing? Who is being breathed?

The "one breath" belongs to us all. As we become this one breath more and more fully, we feel the unutterable connection between us all. I am breathing your breath, you are breathing mine.

Then, when we arise from the experience of oneness on the cushion and walk in kinhin, or engage in other activities, we receive the gift of becoming own unique selves. We cannot walk with our neighbor's feet. We cannot do the work assigned to her. Along with the deep bond of oneness between us, there is also the marvel of uniqueness, of many kinds of different flowers blooming in the garden. Both togetherness and separation are part of the experience of oneness. Both are necessary.

When we live connected to the one breath, when we become able to vividly manifest the unique being we are intended to become, we can also greatly appreciate the uniqueness of other beings. They do not have to turn into us in order for us to appreciate them. We do not have to turn into them.

To focus upon one person as the source of all one's love,

worthiness and security is to deny the true source of love and oneness. This is a fundamental error. Relying on another is an expression of attachment, not love; a manifestation of insecurity and suffering, not understanding the true nature of our lives.

WANTING SPACE TO BREATHE IN

Anna, forty, had been married to Bill for five years. As the years passed, she found herself becoming closer to him. Over time, many of her old single friends dropped away, as did many of his. Outside of work, there was hardly a moment when they weren't together; soon they found it hard to find time to be with their parents and siblings as well. Anna began to fear that they were becoming one person. She wondered how far this could go, if something wasn't wrong. Was she losing her own self and individuality in the process? Had they been wrong to give up their other friends? Bill began to see others as interferences who were jealous of the closeness he and Anna shared. He felt as though they were trying to compete with his relationship, making him feel he was henpecked and that there was something wrong with him.

"What kind of guy makes his wife his best friend?" they told him. "Come on out drinking with the boys."

Bill rejected their invitations and expected Anna to do the same with her family and friends. Anna followed his lead halfheartedly. By now there was barely any space between them, and though she thought she ought to be happy, in truth she began feeling sad.

Anna was involved in a symbiotic relationship with her husband, which made both of their worlds smaller rather than larger and richer. They had created a cocoon between them in which others weren't welcome. They had rejected the world because they were possessive and insecure, which is the opposite of love.

When Anna sought therapy for the situation, the therapist told her she was afraid of love, afraid of the closeness her husband was offering. She had emotional claustrophobia, intimacy problems of the first degree. This didn't resonate with Anna, though Bill quickly agreed. Anna kept feeling there was another way they could experience intimacy and express love that didn't cause their world to shrink, and where there was room for each of them to also live independent lives.

LIVING YOUR OWN TRUTH

Wanting space to grow in is not emotional claustrophobia. An individual who is emotionally claustrophobic begins to feel as though she is suffocating when someone comes too close or begins expressing intense feelings or strong needs for her. She feels as though she is going to be trapped with that person forever, fused, beholden, unable to change or move. Who she is and what she wants for herself will forever be submerged.

Fear of intimacy, or emotional claustrophobia, arises from the deep misunderstanding of what it means to become one with another. It is fostered by the idea that unless the other person is someone we can spar with, keep distance from or dominate, we will be swallowed up, that others are necessarily opposed to us in some way, and we find reasons to run away. This condition was not what Anna was suffering from. She was simply asking for room to be herself.

When she first came to the zendo, Anna was especially struck by the fact that although others were always there, she could be alone at the same time. She had enormous privacy. No one ever intruded upon her thoughts, focus or concentration. What went on inside her was her own business. Each was paying full attention to his own business as well. And yet, a great sense of oneness developed, a sense of love and respect between all those present. Where did it come from? Anna wondered.

As Anna spent more time apart from Bill and grew more self-sufficient, Bill felt abandoned, as though he were losing her. He could not experience oneness when the two of them were physically apart. Any separation for him felt like the end of love. Anna was able to realize that this was not love, but dependency, and that true oneness and love persisted no matter what the external conditions might bring. The more Bill resented her time away from him, the less she wanted to return.

Bill became distressed at the thought of losing Anna. All of his control and possessiveness was to prevent this from happening. However, what we resist we often draw right to our lives. Bill had to be able to deal with parting in order to have a healthy love.

THE FINE ART OF PARTING

In the absolute sense, there is no parting. Yet we meet, touch and have to go. We then suffer so much, feeling that our loved ones are leaving and that we are ultimately alone.

We then fear being close and may even think, "How can I bear to love you if I know that you may go away?" Closeness may then seem like the greatest danger.

We erect so many walls for protection. But living our lives behind these walls we grow lonely and sad; parting, when it does come, hits us even harder then. We missed the chance for the closeness we had.

But until we are able to fully part from a person, we can never dare to love her completely. Most of the time we are stuck in the middle, holding on to the person for dear life, and holding back many things we feel and want to say.

When we learn to be with another without reservation, parting becomes simpler, more natural. We learn how to become complete. When we have not lived fully with her or when we see her as the source of our well-being, her loss can feel like the end of us as well. We fear that once he is gone we will be entirely alone.

BECOMING WHO YOU ARE

Trees, grass and sky all live together. Mountains and clouds live together. Mountain does not obstruct the cloud. Cloud does not obstruct the mountain. Mountain does not become cloud. Cloud does not become mountain. Yet all live together in perfect harmony.

—ZEN TEACHING

When we know who we are and have our true selves, parting is not so difficult. Although there is a sense of loss, we have ourselves to go forward with. Separation from another does not mean the end of our life.

There is a difference between the experience of oneness with all of life and fusion with another person that excludes the rest of the world. True oneness is inclusive and makes the individuality of each person more vivid; it does not imply a loss of one's self, but rather the ability to express and live from who one really is. It does not mean hiding out with another, submerging oneself in a fused situation. This kind of experience can only be painful and extremely limiting.

A crucial step in the process of growing up is developing your own identity, becoming who you are. This happens when we are able to leave our parents, not just physically, but psychologically (and sometimes spiritually) as well. We manifest and honor our own unique selves, the qualities in us that are different from those of our loved ones, qualities that perhaps they may not approve of. For some, becoming independent means rebelling against and rejecting parents. Although this is a common part of the process of self-discovery, the break does not have to last indefinitely, just long enough so that one has the freedom to find who he is—not live his life as an extension of someone else's dreams.

Because the need for independence and personal space of one's own is so deeply intertwined with being in love and with the ability to sustain intimacy in relationships, it must be explored fully. It may be said that we cannot even know what it means to be in love with another until we are at home with ourselves. Before that, our own special gifts and strengths may still not be accessible to us.

It takes courage to become who we are. In order to do this we must yearn to live a life in which we are fundamentally true to ourselves. We risk losing others or their approval of us. When we live from our true selves, however, a new kind of strength comes to us. This strength is not relinquished when we love another, but grows more intense.

Loving another person, becoming one with him, never means relinquishing who we are. This is asked only by those who cannot tolerate differences, who see those who are different from them as inferior or as enemies.

LOSING ONESELF TO FIND LOVE

Evelyn wanted Andrew's love so badly she said she would do anything for it. She changed her hairdo, lost twenty pounds and started wearing the clothes that turned him on. Then it went a step further. She took on his hobbies, went to his church and began finding fault with her own upbringing and beliefs. She saw her family less frequently and spent more time with his.

Although this pleased him at first, later it made him nervous. "The woman I loved isn't here any longer," he said. "I feel as though I'm with a carbon copy of myself."

Soon Andrew no longer found the relationship interesting. Everything became predictable. He lost the sense that there was another person with him in the room.

"Evelyn's being this way made me uneasy," he said. "I always felt alone."

When Andrew broke off the relationship, Evelyn was shattered. She didn't know what she had done wrong, or where to turn now. Beyond that she had little idea who she was anymore.

"I thought this was love," she said, heartbroken. "I thought this was what was meant by becoming closer, two becoming one."

As Evelyn sat in the zendo she felt her own self and strength return. When Andrew saw this, he wanted her back. But Evelyn had no need to return. Right now she was feeling complete and replenished by her practice of zazen.

We must look at the real essence of becoming bonded, becoming one. Losing our sense of self is not it—that is illness. Succumbing to every desire and whim of the other person is not oneness either. Relinquishing responsibility for being who you are is the farthest thing from it. Then what can it be? What is the precious secret of "one breath," no separation, living in universal harmony?

TOUCHING THE MYSTERY

The deepest koan of Zen practice and of our lives is: *Where* does the sense of love, respect and oneness come from? What makes it come to us? What makes it go? When we can answer this incredible question, we will never feel alone again.

Of course most believe that love and respect come as a result of their efforts, that it's up to them to make them happen. The deeper truth is that all we can really do is prepare the ground for love to arise in. We can pull the weeds from our gardens, fertilize the soil, plant the seeds and provide proper conditions—sun, water, shade—then we must allow the love to grow on its own. At some point we must stop hovering around the garden. We cannot keep pulling up the seedlings to see what's going on. By returning to the owner of the garden, we allow the greater harmony to take care of it all. Zen is returning to the owner of our gardens, over and over again. It is honoring and respecting the essential oneness of life that provides and produces nourishment for all. No one is forgotten.

Stepping-Stones to Love
Becoming One

1. KEEPING LOVE AWAY

How do you keep love from coming to you? In what ways do you cause separation between yourself and another person, although you may want to be close? Look at this carefully. Make a list, and be honest about it. It won't hurt just to take a good look.

2. ONENESS

When do you experience your greatest sense of oneness? With a person, alone, at the beach, working, singing, painting, chopping wood, playing cards, listening to music? There is no special rule about where or how this should happen. For each person it is meant to be different. Just locate where it is for you. (Perhaps you haven't yet been aware of it. If not, find out.)

Once you know where you feel the sense of oneness, make a point of spending time there each day. Wherever it is, that is your particular zendo, your place of the one breath. Don't overlook this precious time. Little by little, increase the time you allow yourself to be there, and before you know it, that experience will be with you throughout most of the day.

3. ONENESS WITH OTHERS

Some of us do not allow ourselves to feel oneness with others. It may be too frightening. Others do. Today, choose a person with whom you feel safe enough to allow yourself even a few moments of this precious experience. Make a point of being with that person, and become as quiet as possible in her presence. That is all that is needed. Nothing less, nothing more. Just be there with her, open to her, and expect nothing more of either of you. If she talks to you, listen fully. If she is quiet, be with that. Just accompany her fully. Do this for as long as you can.

This is practice. It is opening the gate, making ourselves as available as possible. During this experience, notice whatever gets in the way. Notice your thoughts, feelings, fantasies, whatever. Just notice them. That's all.

Do this exercise over and over. Pick other people to do it with as well. The more you do it, the softer and more present you will become in the presence of others. (In conjunction with this, don't forget to continue to spend time wherever that experience is most readily available for you.)

4. ONENESS WITH THE ENTIRE WORLD

Find places in your life and in the world where you see division and separation, where you naturally recoil. Stop recoiling. Realize that this is just another manifestation of the one breath. Spend time there, either in person or in your mind. Become aware that wherever you are experiencing separation or aversion is simply part of the universe. Find aspects you could like or approve of. Find aspects that are similar to you. Breathe in and taste your common life force. Let go of your aversion.

5. SERVICE WITH AN OPEN MIND

To truly serve others is to foster the oneness and love between all of life forms. Each day find at least one way you can give of yourself to someone you like, and also to someone you do not care for. Just give fully, forgetting about rewards. The giving itself is the reward. It is preparing your life for love. Forget about yourself in the giving. Just give and then give some more.

You will be amazed at the gifts that will come to you in return, from all sorts of unexpected places. Open your heart and receive them with thanks. This makes the circle complete.

The flower of my life blossoms
When I work to make the flower that is the world.
—UCHIYAMA ROSHI

Chapter 13

FINDING THE OX
(meeting the beloved)

One word frees us from all the weight
and pain of life. That word is love.
—SOPHOCLES

FROM THE MOMENT WE ARE BORN we begin searching for the beloved. In the beginning, we find it in our mother's arms. As we grow older, we turn to father, sister, brother, girlfriends, boyfriends, lovers, teachers, gurus, God. The moment of finding is great indeed. But often the beloved seems to vanish, and when it does, our search resumes instantly. Once we have been in the Garden of Eden, even for a short while, we cannot forget its fragrance and forever long to return.

Some say that finding and losing are the rhythm of life, like day and night, winter and summer, joy and sorrow, hope and despair. This rhythm cannot be altered. We all find and lose the beloved many times in our lives. This is the Tao of life, the force that both brings and takes all things away.

In Zen the longing for the beloved is called "searching for the ox." In the beginning when we come to the zendo we call our quest by different names, but no one really knows what he is searching for. The search for the ox presents itself to different individuals in different ways.

SEARCHING FOR THE OX

In the pastures of this world, I endlessly push aside the
   tall grasses in search of the ox.
Following unnamed rivers, lost upon the interpenetrating
   paths of distant mountains,
My strength failing and my vitality exhausted, I cannot
   find the ox.
I only hear the locusts chirping through the forest at night.
—FROM *ZEN FLESH, ZEN BONES*,
COMPILED BY PAUL REPS AND NYOGEN SENZAKI

There is a universal sense in all of us of having lost something precious in life, and of trying to return to the place where we hope it exists. We often call the object of our search the beloved, or soulmate or perfect person. This longing to return to a place of origination has been described in many traditions. When one has the beloved one feels as though she is in a place of perfection, nirvana, the Garden of Eden.

However, when flaws appear, as they do in all relationships, the beloved is no longer seen as perfectly beautiful, and many feel that they've been tossed out of heaven into a barren world. From the Zen point of view, the loss of our beloved is due to our monkey mind, which talks to us incessantly, ruining the beauty we have found. We constantly see good and evil—we accept the good and reject the evil, but as soon as we see imperfection we are ready to discard the love we have found. At the least provocation we condemn the person and then wonder why we cannot live a life of love.

The Bible says that God looked out at his creation and saw that it was entirely good. God saw only good and therefore all was good to him, plentiful and joyous. This is the mind that does not reject, does not distort or condemn. It is the mind of oneness. This part of ourselves cannot help but love all it sees. This is the way to living a life of love.

Unconsciously, we are all aware that we are vulnerable to moods and influences that scatter and distort our lives, making it bitter and causing us to behave differently from the way we would wish. Sometimes suspiciousness arises in an otherwise fine relationship and sours the situation; other times a person can become unreasonably possessive or jealous of his partner, therefore altering the quality of their time together. Certain individuals decide to hold on to resentment and refuse to forgive. However the negative emotion manifests, we are compelled toward suffering and destruction, of both others and ourselves. The serpent has gotten our ear. Our life becomes a mixture of good and evil. In this kind of environment, love cannot last.

Some would say that this is the fundamental human condition, that living life in love is not only impossible, it is foolhardy, dangerous. Zen disagrees. Living life in love, seeing the beauty in all that appears (in the strong and weak, rich and poor, fierce and gentle) is the only safe and sane way to live. Not only that, the manner in which one perceives the other will affect his life as well. If we dwell upon the ugliness of a person, that person turns ugly before our eyes. If we look for goodness and dwell upon that, the person blooms inevitably.

SEEKING THE RIGHT PERSON

> The perfect ruby we have lost,
> Some say it is to the East of us,
> Others to the West.
>
> —KABIR

Because we do not yet know how to see the beauty in everyone, we search for the perfect person, or perfect mate, believing that there are only a few individuals on this earth that we can truly love. We do this, of course, because our ability to love is limited.

Some who find the one whom they believe to be the perfect person quickly run away. Being with someone we feel is perfect can make us even more painfully aware of our own imagined inadequacies. Deep down we may also believe that this relationship cannot last because we do not really deserve it. Waiting for this rejection to take place can be so painful that some do things to actually bring it about. They show their worst side, pick fights, test the other continually. Anything to get the painful rejection over with! Many destroy the relationship before it sneaks up from behind and destroys them instead.

Is love a game of destroy or be destroyed? Needless to say, this sense of love is bound to bring fear in its trail. The more we are aware of how we unnecessarily shake up our relationships, the easier it is to stop ourselves. We do not have to live our life on automatic pilot, listening to our secret serpents.

Barbara came to the zendo because she felt that the perfect person always eluded her. Each man she met was almost perfect, but not quite there. Something was always missing. Often she could not pinpoint just what was off, but it was something important and she felt it.

Ultimately, the blemishes Barbara saw in others were simply a projection of the way she felt about herself, her feeling that she was shameful, that something was wrong. Barbara's search for another was really a search to make herself complete. Of course no one on the outside could do that because she was already perfect and complete. There was nothing that needed to be added, nothing that could be lost. As soon as she realized that, every person Barbara met would be perfect as well.

We do not honor the spot we stand on. We do not see all that is available right where we are. The illusion has gripped us that someone better is living somewhere else, farther away, that someone better will appear tomorrow, or at another far point in time, that the right person could not possibly be two steps away. We do not see that every person could be the right person, if we looked through the right eyes.

DEMANDING PERFECTION

When she started her Zen practice, Barbara sat on the cushion with difficulty and pain. First her legs hurt, then her back hurt, then her nose itched, then her shoulders grew tight. Because she demanded perfection of herself, she would not give up until she was able to sit there without disturbance. She could never find the right position though. To make matters worse, after zazen, upstairs at tea, she never knew what to say to the other students or to the incredible Zen master. Wrapped in his robes, with his inscrutable glances, he seemed an impossible distance from her. There was the perfect person, she thought, someone she couldn't even greet. Of course she never dared to go see him in dokusan. The distance between them seemed too great.

Finally, after a year of nothing but frustration, just as she was about to leave the zendo, the Zen master nodded to her at tea.

"How are you?" he asked her.

"Terrible," she blurted out. "Everything hurts. Nothing fits together. I'm not getting anywhere. Nothing is perfect."

"That itself is the perfection," he answered quietly.

Barbara broke into a sweat.

The Zen master nodded.

"Thank you," she said.

When everything in the relationship is awkward, doesn't fit, causes irritation, that itself is the perfection. Don't push it away. Don't hate yourself. Don't hate the other. When we can view whatever comes to us as the perfection, before long someone who is right for us will arrive on our doorstep.

Whatever we can't love or accept in another is a mirror of something we can't love or accept in ourselves. We have attracted this person only to see ourselves a little better. What you reject in another, you must also be hiding from and rejecting in yourself.

REALLY LOOK FOR ME

When you really look for me,
you will see me instantly.
—KABIR

When we really look for love we do not run back and forth between this person and that. Instead, we go deeper and look at the nature of love itself. We look at our hunger and our desperation to be filled up. We look at the feeling that we can never be complete, and that there is someone out there who can make us whole.

What is it we dream of? Who we are has never been lost; the love in ourselves is stronger than all the confusion it must confront. We only imagine we are deprived. If we are willing to open our hearts to the love inside and let it come out, it can heal our lives and the lives of others. The mystery is why we will not.

Enyadatta was a Zen student, years ago, who slowly became insane. She had developed the idea that her head was missing and began frantically searching for it. Day after day her search intensified and the more she searched the less she found. Finally, one day a friend brought her to a Zen master, who simply instructed her to sit down in one place, be still and pay attention to her breathing. Hopeless, she had no choice but to comply.

As her wild thoughts quieted down, she was more able to

sit. Little by little, she even forgot the fear she had been living with, the illusion that her head was gone. Then one day an amazing thing happened. Enyadatta suddenly realized that her head was right where it belonged. She jumped up from the cushion, mad with joy. "My head, my head," she began screaming now, "I found it. It's right where it belongs."

Enyadatta realized that nothing was missing. She was perfect, complete and whole. Still, the mad joy she experienced has been described as the Zen sickness—the ecstasy at finding that nothing has been lost, that the doors of the Garden of Eden are always open—we just have to walk in.

When we do not want to love, it is easy to find all kinds of excuses for it by blaming it on the other person. But this is only the fear of love, confusing and distorting our point of view. Once we start loving ourselves, of course, it's an easy step to love another, no matter who he is. Right now, this may feel impossible. Some say they cannot make this jump. The truth is they don't want to. Some even complain that as soon as they decide to be loving, someone comes around and gives them a rough time.

RECEIVING A HARD TIME

Anthony, a new Zen student, complained that the minute he found a relationship, the woman's old boyfriend showed up and tried to get her back. The woman went crazy trying to choose and, inevitably, Anthony lost out.

"It's not worth it," said Anthony, sick of the whole thing. "Love just brings me rotten luck. There's something wrong with all of these women, and there's something wrong with me too."

But hard times are fine. Hard times can be seen as progress, giving a person a chance to confront whatever is between him and being in love. In the middle of a hard time, stop for a minute and ask yourself: Can it really be that there is something wrong with every situation and every person you meet? Are you replaying the same scenario in your life because you are resisting it? Can you accept this hard time completely, just the way it is? Can you step aside and appreciate exactly what's going on? Once you do, things alter.

How can it be that no relationship will ever work for you? These difficulties that appear in our quest for love are like little movies that play themselves out. Don't take them too seriously. Don't get stuck in a reel. Let them roll out and fade away. Do not give them power over you.

THE VOICE OF THE SERPENT

The more we love, or decide to be loving, something odd happens. The serpent arrives, whispers in our ears, and fear comes up to challenge us and lead us astray. Fear can have a life of its own. It can confuse and diminish us or make us run in circles, desperately trying to get away from that which we desire the most. But the farther we run, the tighter the fear holds us in its grip.

Sit or stand quietly and look at the fear. Make its acquaintance. Fear is a bully. As soon as you do not back off, *it* begins to tremble and move away. As soon as we look at the fear directly, it is exposed as the fake it is. Our belief in the fear is what gives it power over us. Rather than believe in the power of fear, why not believe in the power of love? Choose which you would rather believe in.

Another way to tackle the serpent is to ask yourself what you are really afraid of. As we begin to look a little more deeply, we see that the fear of love is never really fear of another. We fear giving of ourselves, opening ourselves, knowing and accepting ourselves just as we are. We fear being known. To love and be loved fully, we must be willing to simply be with another exactly as we are.

Many find that the very act of relinquishing all pretense fills them with love and joy. It is an act of loving and accepting ourselves. This is the basis of all relationship. As you do this, to your delight, other stresses dissolve quickly along with the false front you have been holding on to, and the voice of the serpent fades into the nothingness it came from. Many become braver, freer and more creative. Surprising solutions and insights appear. Other people seem less dangerous and distant. You feel more lovable and awake.

Now with a little patience, it is only a matter of time before the person who knows how to love starts emerging from within. This person knows how to discover the *"right relationship"* and how to thrive in it completely. This is the person who makes friends easily. Isn't it time you let her free?

As this happens, you can now fall in love with everything—beautiful sunsets, rainy days. You do not have to search for love, you are living it, day by day.

TASTING THE FRUITS OF PRACTICE

After students practice for a while they find the burdens of their lives diminishing. Things flow more simply. Where they once found knots they now find their paths clearing. Many also notice their love lives opening up.

"Now when I think of relationships," one student said, "I feel a sense of adventure, as though I cannot pass or fail. Whatever happens, happens. No matter what, I'll enjoy."

The student's sense of herself, her value and beauty is not at stake in each relationship she undertakes. She knows who she is and is at peace with it. She also knows the person who appears before her.

"Many people have been approaching me with offers of blind dates," another student said. "I can't help but feel that the world is full of possibility. I'm not searching for love. It's searching for me."

When we exude a certain energy and vibration, we draw the same into our path. When we are open to enjoying the great adventure of all life, all life becomes open to us as well. In fact, the gates that have been locked inside are now open, and that is why the gates outside are opening as well. When an individual's gates are fully open, she will find herself permanently in love.

In Zen training, when the student finds the ox, it means she finds her true self, the real object of her lifelong search. This phrase is used to describe enlightenment, the attaining of joy and purpose in life, the waking up from the dream of emptiness and separation. This is what most of us seek as we search for our soulmates.

Once the ox has been found, once one has reached the center of their being, stripped away that which is false, they have touched the center of their ability to love. They can now enter the marketplace with "helping hands." These helping hands are open hands, hands truly able to give and receive love. They are not hands which grab, cling, distort or possess, but which are supple, flexible and nurturing. These are the kind of hands and heart needed to live a life of love.

Kabir says, "Fantastic, don't let a chance like this go by!"

Stepping-Stones to Love
Finding the Love You've Been Seeking

1. SEARCHING FOR THE OX
What is the ox that you search for? Where do you believe it can be found? Are you searching to the East or the West?

What has taken place in your search? When did you find it? When was it lost? Take time with these questions. Start to see the search that has propelled your life.

2. EYES OF GOOD AND EVIL

What and whom are you looking at through the eyes of good and evil? What do you see as essentially dangerous about love? Take a moment to turn this around. For a little while, look at it through the eyes of love. See it as beautiful. See it as perfect as it is. Withdraw your condemnation from it. How does this affect you?

3. THE VOICE OF THE SERPENT

What is the voice of the serpent telling you about yourself, love and relationships? What kinds of lies, fears and false reports are being fed into your mind daily that you are believing and buying into? (It is tremendously powerful and empowering to do this exercise.) Whatever we take in unconsciously has great power to direct our lives. Become conscious of the fears, thoughts, fantasies and beliefs that run you that are basically destructive lies. When they arise, tell yourself that it is simply the voice of the serpent talking to you. As soon as you withdraw your belief from them, they dissolve into the smoke they are.

4. THE DIRECT PATH TO LOVE

Give up blame, judgment and condemnation of everyone you meet. We are addicted to this activity. Go cold turkey.

Start becoming aware of how much it runs your life, and each time it surfaces, replace it with a thought of love. Find something positive. Find something beautiful. Turn darkness into light. Look at yourself as if you were looking through the eyes of someone who loved you. Then continue to look at yourself and others that way all day long.

5. THE PERFECT PERSON
Today, really be with whoever crosses your path. Take time to see who she is. Realize everyone is perfect in her own right. (The more you see perfection in others, the more you will see it in yourself.) Open your heart to others today without reservation. Realize there is nothing to fear.

6. FINDING THE OX
Where is your ox (your beloved) today? Where has it been hiding? What made you think you couldn't find it, or wouldn't for a long time? Make friends with the ox. Greet it warmly. Have it enter your life wholeheartedly.

Hundreds of flowers: Spring comes.
For whom do they bloom?
—ZENRIN LEWIS, *THE BOOK OF THE ZEN GROVE*

About the Author

Brenda Shoshanna, Ph.D., is a practicing psychologist, therapist, workshop leader and author. She has published many books, including *Zen Miracles*, *Why Men Leave*, and *Journey Through Illness and Beyond*, winner of the NABE Award for Best Book of the Year in the Category of Health. She is also the relationship expert on iVillage.com and runs workshops nationally on all aspects of psychology, Zen and relationships. Dr. Shoshanna lives in the New York area. Her Web site is www.BrendaShoshanna.com; her e-mail address is Topspeaker@yahoo.com.